ABOUT THE AUTHOR

RONALD MILLAR came to prominence as an author with the publi-
cation of *The Piltdown Men,* a defence of the solicitor Charles Dawson,
the alleged forger of the infamous human fossil from Sussex.

Since then he has written a number of books ranging from biography
and military history to the lives of the Breton tunny fishermen, a venture
in which he was nearly drowned when his sailing schooner was
destroyed in mid-Atlantic by a summer hurricane. Five of the crew per-
ished – only he and the mate survived. 'For a writer there is nothing like
first-hand experience,' he wrote afterwards. 'It should be avoided at all
costs.'

He has also written a number of scripts for stage, films and television
in this country, France, Australia and the United States.

THE GREEN MAN
COMPANION AND GAZETTEER

HIS ORIGINS   HIS HISTORY   HIS FOLKLORE
HIS MEANING   AND WHERE TO FIND HIM

The Forest Spirit from the past with a vital
message for today

Ronald Millar

First published in 1997 by S. B. Publications,
c/o 19 Grove Road, Seaford, East Sussex BN25 1TP

Revised and reprinted 1998
Reprinted 1999
Revised and reprinted 2000
Reprinted 2001

ISBN 1 85770 131 3

Designed and typeset by CGB, Lewes
Printed by MFP Design and Print
Longford Trading Estate, Thomas Street,
Stretford, Manchester M32 0JT

CONTENTS

Page

Foreword	6
THE START OF THE QUEST	7
1 THE CROSS AND THE SACRED GROVE	11
2 THE SPIRIT OF THE WILDWOOD	21
3 THE GOOD GOD GUIDE	31
4 WHERE TO LOOK	39
5 ENGLISH FOLKLORE AND THE GREEN MAN	47
6 THE GREEN MAN IN LITERATURE	69
7 GREEN MAN GAZETTEER	79
Bibliography	86
The Company of the Green Man	87

ACKNOWLEDGEMENTS

The author wishes to acknowledge his indebtedness to the late Kathleen Basford for her beautiful photographs and to Angela King of *Common Ground*, a selfless, non-profit making charity dedicated to the preservation of the peace and traditions of our countryside. He would also like to thank photographer Karen Pratt of Steyning for her back cover picture of the sign at the Green Man, Jolesfield, Partridge Green, West Sussex and to thank Barbara and Alan Marsh of the Post Office at Steyning for their kindness in allowing the interruption in the flow of their business so that Karen could get at their Green Man.

Front cover: The Green Man in all his glory, but an early fifteenth century craftsman has omitted the foliage from his mouth so making him a *tete de feuilles*.

FOREWORD

THE GREEN MAN – MOTIF AND MAGICIAN

THESE are times of Man's deep conflict with his environment, of polluted water courses and concreted countryside, and if the Green Man had not already been in existence then something very like him would have been invented. He is the perfect icon for all who recognise that in Progress we risk losing something vital to our well-being, our survival even, call these sentient folk 'green', environmentalists, conservationists, Common Ground, Men of the Trees or what you will.

Two millennia old or older, the Green Man is the vibrant spirit of the wild wood, of vegetation in leaf or bud, of spring, pool and river, earth and sky, indeed the totality of Nature. His voice is the hiss of high wind in ash and oak. And his profundity those sudden silences of a forest when all Nature seems to hold her breath. When we hear or feel him no more mankind will have run its course.

THE START OF THE QUEST

FIRST meetings with the Green Man are usually by accident rather than design. For the late Kathleen Basford, one of the early inquirers into the riddle of the Green Man, it began one bleak winter's day in Yorkshire. Wandering through the ruins of Fountain's Abbey she happened to glance upwards and saw the only human touch in the mass of grey stonework. At the apex of the window arch was a sad, old, withered stone face which disgorged a weird growth of vegetation from the stone mouth.

She was to discover that the head had been inserted some time in the fifteenth century to make good a gap in the masonry due to settlement down the centuries. By now she knew the head with foliage sprouting from mouth, nose, eyes, was an established motif in church decoration but she was surprised at his arrival at Fountains, home of an austere order of Cistercian monks for whom any kind of decoration was abhorrent.

This bizarre intrusion was the stuff of legend. The strange old man caught up in his stone branches was a ghost from the past who brought a deeper sadness to the old grey abbey walls. She called him a Green Man for convenience but surely this image of sorrow and death could have nothing to do with the jolly Jack in the Green of maypoles and May Day revels or with the Church's interpretation as a figure of joy and resurrection.

Mrs Basford was right to be puzzled. He seemed to be all three. He was also an echo of a powerful Celtic god belonging to the pantheon celebrated by those men of mystery, the Druids. What had he to do with the religion of the Virgin and Child? She wondered what the head in the leaves might have suggested to the humble wood carver or stone mason. Was he ever given a free hand, allowed to make what he liked of such work, so that his appearance was accidental, perhaps due to a pot of ale too many down the road.

The fifteenth century Green Man corbel in St Jerome's church, Llangwm, that prompted Lady Raglan to suspect an association with the folklore figure, Jack in the Green.

The title of her subsequent book *The Green Man* is misleading. She weighs the problem dispassionately, fairly, then reaches the reluctant conclusion that there was no connection at all between the church figure and the jolly Jack in the Green.

But there had been no doubt about the association in the view of Lady Raglan and she had said so in a manner worthy of a descendant of the family responsible for the Charge of the Light Brigade.

Her acquaintance with the Green Man began in 1939 when Western Europe was slipping inexorably into a deadlier conflict, one which was to make her ancestor's Crimean War seem like a lover's tiff. The parson at St Jerome's church at LLangwm in Monmouthshire, now called Gwent, drew her attention to a carving in the choir formerly concealed by a fifteenth century rood screen. Another was carved on a corbel. No faces of misery or capitulation these but bold implacable ruffians ejecting acanthus fronds from their mouths as if doing so was all in a day's work.

The Reverend J Griffiths suggested the figures might represent 'inspiration' but Lady Raglan heartily disagreed. There was no doubt that here was the Green Man of rural tradition by some mysterious process, who knows what or why, translated into the House of God. She wrote in *Folklore* magazine that:

> ... the question is whether there was any figure in real life from which it [the Llangwm example] could have been taken. The answer, I think, is there is only one of sufficient importance, the figure known variously as the Green Man, Jack in the Green, Robin Hood, the King of the May, and the Garland, who is the central figure in the May Day celebrations throughout northern and central Europe.

Her contribution was not entirely original. Others had thought the same but it is generally agreed that it was Lady Raglan's uncompromising declaration that gave the ecclesiastical figure the name Green Man.

Formerly he had been known timorously by a variety of names including foliate head, grotesque, or gargoyle. The French cautiously called him *tete de feuilles*

The master mason Villard de Honneourt made notes and drawings, now in the *Bibliotheque Nationale*, of the foliate heads he saw in the cathedrals and churches of thirteenth century France. He labelled them all, mask and men, *Tete de Feuilles*.

9

(head of leaves), *masque feuilles* (leaf mask) or, slightly more daring, *le feuil-lu* (the leafy one). It was *blattmaske* (leaf mask) for the Germans, too, but in Germany the leaf colour, *grune,* covered individuals performing ancient folk rituals under various guises, one party of revellers actually being called *Der Gruner Mensche.*

It would be as well to confess my own Road to Damascus, no fifteenth century Welsh church or ancient abbey cloisters for me but the queue in the post office at Steyning in West Sussex.

Short of something to look at I glanced upwards and saw a curious spider-like figure looking down on me from the roof beam above my head. It has an imp's face with long, spindly branches sprouting from its cheeks. I had read that something very like him was carved on a bench end in St Mary's church, Bishops Lydeard, Somerset. **(See page 85)**

The post office is a very old building but the elegant piece of polished timber of the Green Man carving seems even older, perhaps from the Swann Inn that stood on the site in the seventeenth century.

'Did you know that there's a Green Man on that beam?' I asked the woman behind the counter, as if reporting the discovery of America.

'Nothing serious, I'm sure,' she snapped, perhaps thinking that I was talking about a variety of dry rot and was fearful of the roof's imminent collapse.

It was a magical moment all the same. My quest began.

The Green Man on one of the beams in Steyning Post Office. *Photo: Karen Pratt.*

1

THE CROSS AND THE
SACRED GROVE

THE King's commonsense counsel to Alice to begin at the beginning then go on to the end then stop does not apply to the Green Man. The Green Man has no discernible beginning – and when it appears he is at an end he bursts into life as 'innovative' decoration or as an icon for those who fear the despoliation of the countryside.

But where might have he begun? An early candidate resolutely put up as an original Green Man is the Egyptian god Osiris, just because he is the god of fertility and his face is painted green in the tomb of Nefertari. While we are at it we might as well include Eve and her fig leaf. But a far better forerunner is Dionysius, Greek god of wine and whoopee, always depicted with leafy beard and branches growing out of his head, symbolic of his role of god of trees in general. The Romans, notorious copycats, faithfully replicate him as Bacchus, similar appearance, similar role.

The Romans had a tradition of popping carved leaf breakers into monumental inscriptions, a combined good luck charm and punctuation, apparently to assure the gods of the purity of the dedication. Metal leaves were also important for invoking the participation of the gods in one's private affairs. The leaf was inscribed with the curse, blessing or wish and thrown into a pool or spring dedicated to the deity considered the most appropriate, dropping the priest a denarius or so for his trouble. The leaves could be anything from lead to silver, the more precious the metal the more potent the spell.

The Green Man's most rudimentary form is a leaf incised or marked on

11

stone or wood with a few lines to suggest eyes, nose and mouth. The next phase is the leaf mask, like the weepers of Neumagen. This kind have been discovered from Bath to Baalbek, some with snakes in their hair or seaweed beards, as far detached from the spirit of the greenwood as might be imagined.

But leaf masks without distracting elements are to be found on the second century triumphal arch of Septimus Severus and Aurelian's Temple of the Sun in Rome. Another is carved on the facade of a temple to Bacchus at Al Hatra in Iraq. The Roman armies took the Green Man with them wherever they went.

It is a pity that the Green Man cannot speak for himself but on the singular occasion he did– or rather the sculptor spoke for him by carving 'Silvanus' above his head – it prompted an acrimonious scholastic debate which generated more heat than light. This particularly troublesome example is a one of a number of heads of Roman deities carved round the rim of a drinking fountain at the abbey of Saint-Denis, Seine.

A faction suggested that there was no such entity as a Green Man, that in fact he was the deity known to the Romans as Silvanus under another name and the fountain carving was proof of it.

'How can there be a Green Man when he is called Silvanus?' they challenged. 'But how can he be Silvanus when he has a crown of leaves?' demanded the other. The Romans were most particular about the correct appearance and appurtenances of their gods and Silvanus was half mortal, half goat and carried a cypress branch symbolic of his hopeless love for Cyparissus, a shepherd boy. That the head was carved in the twelfth century and that it was a head only so he might have been half pig and carried an umbrella as far as anybody knew was an irrelevance in such rarified academic circles. The crown of leaves was proof of his imposture and proved his undoing.

Ignoring the more contentious issues it seems certain that the Green Man was given birth somewhere in the Mediterranean basin. And archaeologists agree that he has been with us a long time, perhaps evolving, changing in meaning, intention, style, as the centuries pass. Whether in his original form he was purely decorative or had deeper significance is unknown. And whether he meant the same both north and south of the Alps or was the result of two entirely separate inspirations or whether one influenced the other also remains a mystery.

Learned talk of 'influences' sounds fine but means little and a half dozen experts are likely to produce at least as many opinions, usually more. Far better to be one's own expert, stick to the empirical and reliable principle that if he looks like a Green Man then he probably is one and leave the decorations of pyramids and Hindu temples alone. Artistic nuances on the banks of the Nile a few thousand years ago may have caused pharaoh's wife to swoon but impact on a rustic woodcarver in the heart of medieval England is likely to be slight. Asked whether his work was Osiristical or Bacchanalian old Jack would say he preferred cheddar.

The Green Man with foliage sprouting from his mouth or emerging from other facial orifices seems to be unique to north western Europe and little like those elsewhere – the Mediterranean basin, China or North Borneo, for instance. This is a personal assessment.

Another is that the Green Man in his infinite variety is at the very heart of Old England. One feels comfortable in his company although sometimes he loves to frighten. He beckons us down some fascinating and unfrequented paths of discovery, into cool, dim churches among the alabaster and marble tombs of forgotten men and women. There he waits, hidden in shadow or subtly lit by the sparkling jewels of old stained glass.

But first, despite what has been said, it is necessary to take a brief imaginary excursion over the Channel, across France to Neumagen on the Mosel, just outside the ancient south German city of Trier, the one-time capital of Constantine the Great and hub of the Christian faith.

Here the Green Men are instantly recognisable and they are reckoned to have

A kingly Green Man depicted in fourteenth century stained glass in St Mary Redcliffe church, Bristol

13

The weeping Green Men of Neumagen cemetery.

been carved roughly at the same time as those on the triumphal arches in Rome. The heads are on the splendid tombs of wealthy burgers, wine producers and exporters and their families, and the masons seem to have enjoyed their work for not a few of the carvings on the tombs show the crews of wine ships the worse for sampling the cargo. Not so the Green Men.

As a contrast to the jolly drunken sailors, barrels of wine, amphorae and baskets of fruit, the squashed heads weep. Kathleen Basford was prompted to exclaim: 'How can a cluster of leaves seem so grief-stricken?' How indeed.

Like the Roman heads they vary in style. Some faces are completely veiled by acanthus leaves with leaves growing from tear ducts. Others have leafy brows and beards and some have the human aspect, eyes, noses, mouths, merely suggested by folds in leaves.

These sculptures are important in the Green Man 'first' game for they mark his earliest appearance north of the Alps, most likely a theme imported when the clever idea of growing grapes and making wine from them was brought there from Rome

Another famous 'first' came to light a hundred years ago at Trier Cathedral when a masonry screen was removed during renovations. These magnificent Green Men were hidden for almost a thousand years, imperious individuals, crowned with acanthus and with acanthus beards and moustaches. Casts were made for the city museum then they were returned to the sleep which had overtaken them in the eleventh century. A 'window' was left so that at least one of the heads can be seen.

The Green Men, carved on four faces of hefty blocks of stone, are capitals of pillars raised in the sixth century by Bishop Nicetius who rebuilt the cathedral after yet another burning by barbarian marauders, on that occasion by the Franks, a Germanic tribe spreading south from somewhere between the Rhine and the North Sea. Two centuries later they overran Gaul to change its name to France. A few are said to have followed through into Britain.

The gods of the Franks were far older than the Christian one celebrated by the good bishop. They were Celts and theirs was the reli-

A cast of one of the heads salvaged from a Roman temple and walled up for centuries in Trier Cathedral.

gion of the Celtic Iron Age, that of the Druids and one wonders what came over Nicetius for him to bring pagan Green Men into his cathedral, second-hand stock, pillaged from a local second century Roman temple. This was confirmed in the 1960s when an archaeological dig revealed gaps in the masonry from which the heads had been snitched.

Perhaps Nicetius admired the workmanship of the heads or perhaps, stealing a march on later generations, he believed that they represented rebirth or resurrection. He must have thought the intrusion harmless enough but whatever his reason he was the first to bring Green Men into the service of the Christian faith.

And he was the first to the bring into confrontation the icons of two bitter adversaries – the crucifix of monks dressed in wool habits who followed the teachings of the son of a humble but eloquent Jewish carpenter and the Green Man adored not only by Romans but by white-robed mystics who worshipped spirits of air, earth and water in sacred groves.

15

It is just possible however that the good bishop considered the heads were trophies of war, a custom dear to the heart of the Celts of old. He could not be unaware of the grim battle being waged outside the walls of his city with reinforcements of holy lumberjacks from other lands. Stripped to the waist and spitting on their hands they turned up in droves, nameless monks and great Supermen for Christ such as Saint Martin of Tours and the Devonian, Saint Boniface, from . . . could it be Crediton?

This carving in the church at Codford St Peter, Wiltshire could be interpreted as a holy lumberjack. either St Boniface or St Martin, punishing a druidical grove

The Old Religion was well entrenched and would be next to impossible to shift but the saintly thugs were no slouches. They promoted poisonous anti-Druid propaganda and set about destruction of the sacred groves, centres of continuing Druidical influence. The battle communiques called *Lives of the Saints* are full of marvels and miracles and either the monks who wrote them were crazy or God's interference in human affairs has declined enormously.

Confronting a much worshipped pine tree Saint Martin ordered it cut down and had no fear when the Druid guardian agreed – providing the saint stood in its path. Nigh unto death by squashing the saint made the sign of the cross and the tree rose again and dropped on his rival instead.

His brother holy axe wielder was Saint Boniface, a Briton from Devon. His story does not end happily. His miraculous gift was to cause Druidical oaks to burst into minute atoms then reform in the shape of the True Cross.

He made holy sawdust and converted pagans right across north west Europe but was martyred at last by an exasperated tree worshipper who was even quicker with the axe.

It is not unlikely that Boniface developed his horror of Druids in his native county of Devon, one of their last strongholds. The old name for the open-air cathedrals where they conducted their ritual is *nemeton*, meaning 'sacred grove'. This is echoed in the names of no less than five Devon villages, all within a stone's throw of where the post holes of a Druidical 'woodhenge' have been located, most likely the *nemeton* for which the villages were named. Pertinently, most of the parish churches have dozens of frightening Green Men keeping the parishioners in order and at least two churches were originally dedicated to Saint Martin of Tours, he of the self-raising pine.

Sometimes these saintly contests with Evil seemed like an Olympic decathlon. One can almost see the banners, hear the cheers and counter-cheers of the rival factions. There was some attraction about the tops of mountains or hills and the most famous event of all was held on the summit of Mont-Dol in northern Brittany and it was Archangel Michael versus the Devil himself. There was swordplay, running, leaping, wrestling, putting the rock, singing, dancing, poetry, harping and flying. Saint Samson was referee, a rash concession on the part of the competitor in the red strip for the monk unsportingly adjudged Michael the winner. The silver-medallist flew off with a howl of fury, leaving his claw marks on the north-eastern hump that people can see to this day.

Pope Gregory cautioned his often over-zealous missionaries to go gently, writing to Saint Augustine:

'Do not pull down the temples. Destroy the idols, purify the temples with holy water, set [holy] relics there and let them become temples of the True God.'

It seems that this restraint did not apply to sacred groves and the muscular saints were not the meek and mild psalm singing and praying kind that one reads about in the scriptures. They had to contend, physically as well as philosophically, with devils and dragons and evil spirits – aphorisms for Druids and their henchmen who strove just as courageously and cannily to preserve the Old Religion. Unswerving in zeal to save pagan congregations from Hell they mercilessly snuffed out all ritual that could not be remodelled to serve the religion of Christ.

They cheated, turned troublesome Druidical gods and festivals into

Thirteenth century corbels of Green Men. This one, on St Mary's church, Wadenhoe, Northants, has a bad eye.

Centuries of erosion have given the corbel on St Wulfram's church, Grantham, a fearsome dog with bone expression

The masonry supporting this thirteenth century corbel in the cathedral at Ripon gives this Green Man the appearance of a sergeant in the French Foreign Legion.

Dorchester Abbey, Oxfordshire. A figure of eight mouth lends unbending cruelty to the features on this corbel.

Christian ones. In fact they had little choice about the festivals for they were dictated by nature's clock plus essential life-preserving customs such as autumnal slaughter of cattle against the famine of winter. Some believe that the Celtic calender was ordained by agriculture – the germination of seed, ripening of crops, harvest and so on. While others are sure that as being at first migrant herdsmen they based it on animal husbandry such as birth of lambs and lactation of ewes. The classical historian Lucretius is firmly on the side of the pastoralists, writing:

> And this [Celtic] race of men from the plains were all the harder, for hard land had bore them; built on stronger and firmer bones, and endowed with mighty sinew, they were a race undaunted by heat or cold, plague, strange new foodstuffs. For many years among the beasts of the earth they led their life. And none was yet a driver of the curved plough or could turn the soil with iron blade, nor bury a new shoot in the ground nor prune the ripened branch from the tree.

Most likely it evolved like most other things to serve both. Whatever, there is general agreement that the start of the Druidical year was not January but at the Feast of Samhain which falls in November. The Christians called it All Saints. And all agree on the importance to Christian and Druid alike of the Beltane festival on May Day to celebrate the coming of spring and rebirth of the earth, the day of Jack in the Green and Morris dancers. And they are in concord about the feast of the summer solstice on or about June 21, now celebrated by modern Druids and New Age travellers in conflict with constabulary on Salisbury Plain. And Lughnasadh which is the Celtic harvest festival.

Modern farmers are inclined to sniff at these festivals which were celebrated with enormous bonfires. 'Reminders of the human sacrificial fires', hint the enemies of the Druids darkly. The author was told by one (farmer not Druid) that he needed no guidance of the kind. Sheep had no doubt when to mate and the farmer knew when the land and prevailing weather were ready for sowing and when crops were ripe to harvest.

'Sow on the wax, reap on the wane and you can't go far wrong' he added phlegmatically, ruining his argument with his dependence on phases of the moon and going back to the lore of the Druids.

2

THE SPIRIT OF THE WILDWOOD

The Greeks and the Romans were fond of temples in sylvan glades but their sophisticated rusticity seems too fragile for the dense wildwood of north west Europe. This is a major consideration in the argument that the classical leaf masks or foliate heads of Rome may have little in common, not only in appearance but meaning, with the more robust Green Man.

Well into this millenium much of Europe was still covered with dense primaeval forest in which, as Sir James Fraser comments in his classic study of magic and religion *The Golden Bough*, the scattered clearings must have seemed like islets in an ocean of green. The tribes whom Caesar encountered on his military campaigns scarcely knew what he meant when he asked where the trees ended. One might travel for months without reaching their limit, he was told.

According to this famous general the wildwood was haunted by curious and unnatural beasts, the unicorn being one. He remarks that some of the creatures had been seen to lean against trees, the allusion lost until it is realised that this is the habit of a two not a four legged beast and Caesar was hinting that they were centaurs – the half man, half bull of legend. Or Pan himself. Four centuries later another emperor, Julian, was complaining about the depressing solitude, gloom and silence of the endless greenery. He said he knew nothing like it in the whole of the vast Roman Empire.

The Weald of Kent, Sussex and Surrey, is all that remains of the once continuous woodland that sprawled over most of southern England. In the west it joined the trees which stretched into Devon. When early

This Green Man in All Saints' church, Sutton Benger, Wiltshire has features that suggest the untamed spirit of the wildwood.

Stonehenge was erected most likely it was surrounded by trees despite the romantic picture of Druids watching the sun come up over the Heel Stone on Midsummer's Day, unless, of course, they were late risers.

When Henry ll's knights slew Archbishop Thomas Becket in front of the High Altar at Canterbury wild bull and wild boar were still hunted in the woods outside the walls of London. When Richard Crookback lost his crown to Henry Tudor on Bosworth Field he also lost no less than sixty eight royal forests. And it was said that a squirrel could leap from tree to tree throughout the entire length of Warwickshire.

Small wonder then that trees played an omnipresent part in the lives of those who lived in such a densely forested land, that it was widely believed that trees and plants had souls just like people and should be treated accordingly. Plutarch tells a nice story of villagers dashing back and forth with buckets of water as though fighting a fire just because a sacred tree was wilting.

Treating trees as human oracles and consulting with them over important matters was common and so was the planting and care of sacred groves where to break of a single branch brought bad luck with death or crippledom. A particularly revolting penalty was exacted in Germany where the culprit's stomach was slit and entrails fastened to the wounded tree and he or she driven round the trunk until death intervened.

The concept that trees and plants were part of the community led to them being treated as male and female. On Christmas Eve fruit trees were 'married' with straw ropes in the belief that they would produce a heavier crop. And just as widespread was the belief that the tree was the temporary lodge of a spirit which could at will vacate it and wander abroad as a forest god. In art this transformation was depicted as a change to human form, a woodland deity became man or woman holding a leaf or some other symbol or clue to their identity, as in the cypress of Silvanus. Later his head is a leaf mask, later still entirely the Green Man.

When Saint Jerome set about persuading the new converts to destroy their sacred groves they complained that by doing so they would also destroy the home of the spirits which brought sunshine, rain and caused the crops to grow and which fattened cattle – a fear not without foundation today. They too firmly believed in the beneficence of woodland and the malevolence of those who wish to destroy it. But in contradiction there were customs that involved the cutting down instead of the veneration of trees. One rite that immediately comes to mind is of course the Christmas Tree, said to be Victorian or, if not, certainly a comparatively recent tradition.

Where this 'recent' myth arose is unknown but the tree ritual is of enormous age, far older than the Feast of Saint Stephen when the Druids called it something else. Similarly presumed lost in the mists of pre-Christianity are the May Day festivities which the Druids called Beltane, undoubtedly one of the oldest and most famous festivals of all.

In spring or early summer or even on Midsummer's Day it was the custom in the remoter parts of these islands to go into the woods, cut down a tree and bring it back to the village where it was set up to general rejoicing. A variation on the same theme, one kinder to the tree, was to just bring back branches to be nailed to gateposts and celebrated in a similar way.

According to Fraser the intention was to bestow the blessing of the tree spirit or forest god on the household. A variation was the planting of a may tree in front of every house or a visit was paid to each by a procession carrying a tree. In this 'dressing of the village' by procession the origins of the morris dance will be found, together with our Green Man or Jack in the Green, Lord of the May or Greenwood, call him what you will.

Oddly, morris dancers are often strangely reluctant to admit the vast age of their ritual dance. 'Not any older than the Crusades,' said the bagman of one side, a casual dismissal of seven centuries which knocked the breath out of an inquirer from the United States.

Perhaps this reticence over its antiquity is as traditional as the ritual itself, a means of slipping under the guard of a vigilant and jealous Church, the acknowledgement of too vast an age suggesting pagan origins.

History has the habit of being written by the victor who naturally finds little good to say about the loser. Most of what we know about the mortal enemy of the Christians suffers in this respect. But some idea of what the Druids were about has survived. These holy men of the Dark Ages needed no churches or temples but worshipped in the open air, forest clearings, by pools and rivers, streams and springs. They are said to have wielded absolute power over the lives of non-Druids, there being no clear dividing line between religion, culture and everyday

A Tree of Life in the church at Roslin, near Edinburgh, believed to be mid fifteenth century.

activities. This mix of temporal and secular authority would have the Archbishop of Canterbury turning up at Twickenham to put a stop to a rugger international because he did not like the song the supporters were singing, or hated white jerseys

The priests were judges, lawmakers, philosophers, physicians, bards and possibly there was even a warrior caste. They could at whim condemn to death or excommunicate and a man deprived of tribal protection was hunted down like a wild animal. It might be as well to remember that these powers were not much different from the draconian forestry laws of medieval England where being declared 'wolfshead' meant an offender could be killed on sight. Bands of such outlaws haunted the denser forests and gave rise to the enchanting tales of Robin Hood and his jovial company and his constant pulling the nose of the wicked Sheriff of Nottingham.

Neither Robin nor the sheriff were real historical characters. Robin Hood's name is thought to derive from Robin in the Hood and together with his green clothing is a direct allusion to his real persona as the Green Man of folklore. The signboards of the numerous public houses named the Green Man (there are over thirty in London alone) almost without exception show him as Robin Hood. One exception is at the Green Man and French Horn in St Martin's Lane in London where he is actually the woodland spirit. That Robin was popular with the people is manifest from the repeated theme that he robbed the rich to feed the poor. The earliest legends know him as Robin Goodfellow – more insubstantial woodland sprite than a human being – a Church name for the Green Man when it did not feel threatened.

The Druids committed their lore and ritual to memory during long years of study at regular academies, one account suggesting that up to nineteen years were necessary for the higher offices. The largest was probably at Arras in France, or Gaul as it was called then, although the chief religious centre was said to be in Britain, somewhere in the West Country but not indisputably Stonehenge.

The Druids wrote in Old Celtic, which is not surprising, but also in Latin and Greek. This they did sparingly, preferring feats of memory to train the intellect for philosophical deliberations. Unkindly it was said that the real reason for this reluctance to commit anything to writing was to prevent obscure predictions being revealed as meaningless mumbo-jumbo, a ruse not entirely unheard of in modern fortune tellers. But we have it on no less than the authority of the great historian, Pliny, that they did wear white robes and ritually cut mistletoe with golden sickles. If that were not enough, folk tradition is unshakeable on this point.

Pliny wrote that the mistletoe was a good plant for healing and particularly efficacious if cut according to a prescribed ritual. Then he mentions that two white bulls are essential as well. The white-robed priest climbs to the top of the oak, attacks the mistletoe with a golden sickle and when it falls it must be caught in a white robe by those standing below. Then the bulls are sacrificed.

The Druids believed that the souls of the dead passed into other forms, human, animal or vegetable, in a kind of continuing chain of immortality. There was no equivalent of a Christian purgatory or Hell with roasting for the wicked after death but instead a land of perfect happiness variously called the Otherworld, the Land of Eternal Youth, the Isle of the Blessed or something similarly attractive. Some accounts describe these heavens as hells, the haunts of imps, demons and the tortured souls of the damned, but this is almost certainly Christian scare tactics inserted later to discourage backsliders.

For the Druids the Otherworld was similar to the Norse Valhalla where time has no meaning in earthly terms. A year might last a minute or a minute an eternity. It

A bench end in the church at Crowcombe, Somerset, an area with strong traditional associations with a warring dragon, a Church aphorism for Druids.

26

is a place of undiluted pleasure, of perpetual happiness with non-stop music, feasting, drinking, sexual romps and other social activities dear to the Celtic heart, unlimited brawling and opportunities for heroic death. Death and wounds were no hardship for one returned to full health and vigour on the following day.

Faith in this happy happy land was so entrenched and widespread that Caesar's Celtic enemies, even the renegades that fought for him, were without fear, even determined to die at the earliest opportunity, provided more immediate earthly pleasures did not intervene. They burnt, slew, looted, raped, without reck or ruth, attacking stark naked, a battle, it seems, resembling a fire at a nudist colony.

The scene of the final conflict in warrior-queen Boudicca's rebellion against the Romans is as described by Tacitus in correct nightmare terms:

> The Druids were ranged in order, with hands uplifted, invoking the gods, and pouring forth horrible imprecations. The novelty of the sight struck the Romans with awe and terror. The Britons perished in the flames which they themselves had kindled. The island, [Inez Mons then, now Anglesey] fell, and a garrison was established to retain its subjection. The religious groves, dedicated to superstition and barbarous rites, were levelled to the ground.

If Ceasar, Strabo and Pliny are to be believed, the Druids were given to frightful religious rites which were the terror of the living. No strangers to cruelty and bloodletting themselves the Romans were horrified, at least they said they were. Caesar stressed that the main reason behind the Roman conquests was to put an end to the Druids and their ritual carnage, a solid excuse for annexation which, with variations, modern tyrants find useful. The killings included mass human sacrifice by burning in colossal wicker images of the deity of the month, ordeals by fire and water and the placation of gods with the offer of human heads. The worst annual slaughter was at Samhain to propitiate the spirits in hope of survival through the harsh, barren months of winter.

An unpleasant variant of the crystal ball is described by Strabo who explains:

> They used to strike a man whom they have dedicated to death in the back with a knife and then divine [the future] from his death throes, but they did not sacrifice without a Druid. We are told of other kinds of sacrifices, for example they would shoot victims to death with arrows or impale them within their temples.

This may imply that the Druids got someone else to do the killing for them, one not so black spot in an otherwise gruesome record. And when the Romans had finished it was the turn of the monks, similarly undispassionate and non-objective, determined to contrast the sanctity of their side with the evil of their adversaries.

The starved and weary monks often lost track of whom they were supposed to be exalting, confused Druid with monk, one religion with the other, even writing of a freezing Hell. In one instance this confusion preserves the name of a Druid, an almost unique event.

His name was Kian Gwenc'hlan, meaning Kian of the White Race, possibly an allusion to his Druidical robes although the Druids did use 'gwen' or 'white' for their holy ground. The monks countered with 'white' for their churches, hence the frequent occurrence in England with variations on Whitechurch or Whitchurch.

Kian lived on Menez Bre, a small mountain in Brittany, and he was blind, a bard, a prophet and he stole horses. Another dweller on the mountain was a devout monk named Machoarvien, a name which the French could not get their tongues round so it was changed to Hervé.

Saint Hervé is patron protector of horses although he too was a horse-thief for, the monk adds cheekily, his birthplace assured him of that for there horse-thievery was imbibed with mother's milk. A strange quality in a holy man, particularly a blind one for the monk chronicler now announces that Herve was similarly afflicted. We now have two blind horse-thieves living in the same hermitage on the same mountain.

One day Hervé confronts Kian and attempts to convert him to Christianity. The Druid replies that if the monk persists in his gospel chatter he will utter a curse and all the Christian chapels in the land will fall down. This badly scares the monk and he leaves the Druid to his 'paganism'. The preservation of the churches of France by not pestering Kian is reason enough for the monk to ascribe sainthood to Hervé.

On 17 June, within a few days of the summer solstice and feast of the sun god Belinus, a prayer at the chapel of Saint Hervé on Menez Bre will cure a sick horse. If a crippled child is bathed in Kian's Spring at the chapel he or she will be cured.

Horse-thievery and blindness of both monk and Druid is strange imagery and the implication lost. However, the tale is typical of a legend getting a dose of Christian disinfectant and, by the poor monk losing the thread of his tale, the Druid coming off best.

A carving at Poitiers of perhaps the fourth or fifth century exemplifies the confused overlap of the Old and New Religions. A Green Man certainly, but he appears on the marble tomb of a woman – Sainte-Abre.

In appearance he is not unlike the figures at Steyning (see page 10) and Bishops Lydeard (see page 83) of much later times except the leafy branches grow from his nostrils, a departure from a tradition that would be adhered to consistently throughout the Middle Ages, so much so that one wonders whether clenching a leafy branches between the teeth was a Druidical fetish, one unmentioned by historians, ancient or modern.

A large leafy branch is clenched firmly between the teeth of this figure on a medieval misericord in the cathedral at Southwell, Nottinghamshire.

Saint Abre was the daughter of Saint-Hilaire, one of the early missionaries to the Gauls, yet the carving is said to represent him not her. But why a saint is depicted as a Green Man and what a celibate monk is doing with a daughter remains a mystery. And there are other imponderables. Is this really the tomb of a saint or is he a Druid? And it seems a mighty coincidence that Abre is just one letter removed from 'arbre', both French and Gallic for 'tree', in this context meaning 'holy tree'.

The monks were not only in deep conflict with Druids but with themselves. Celtic monks who had held sway since before the Romans soldiers arrived were now faced with a new breed of monk from Rome.

The Celtic monks were Druidical in their preoccupation with the astronomical calender. The Roman monks held no brief for such survivals and roundly condemned feasts contaminated by pagan gods like the Green Man.

So different were these religious philosophies that sometimes Roman monks celebrated Easter while Celtic monks were still at their Lenten fast. And there was bitter dispute over the tonsure. Celtic monks shaved forehead and skull back to the ears to imply intellectualism while the Romans were content with shaving the crown, seemingly a minor matter but this and similar controversies threatened to sunder the entire Church establishment.

The Celts gave up in the end and crept away to remote hermitages on barren cliffs and small storm-swept islands and Rome reigned supreme.

And the Green Man inherited an undivided and implacable enemy.

3

THE GOOD GOD GUIDE

THE Celtic slave clutched at his new master's military robe. 'Don't cross the river here,' he pleaded. 'On the other side wait the Hawthorn Queen and the Heron King.'

'I care nothing for such superstitions,' said the Tribune, turning in his saddle to wave his cohorts forward. And the Roman Army went on to win the Battle of Brentwood despite the evil omen.

To honour the hero the Senate accorded him a full Triumph. He was permitted to march his legion into Rome under its eagles, carrying weapons, with fanfares, beating drums and carts piled high with the spoils of the great victory. To demonstrate to the citizens of Rome the extent of his valour with his manacled captives from Britain strode two actors, one bedecked with may blossom the other striding along on stilts, in feathered cloak and with a long wooden beak fastened over his face. They too were in chains but much lighter ones and they were giving their employer his money's worth in theatrical terror and weeping.

'See how the pagan gods tremble before the might of Rome. What price now the precious Hawthorn Queen and Heron King?' thundered the priest over the tumult, holding the ceremonial laurel leaf above the general's brow. To the Senate's utter astonishment the captives suddenly erupted into uncontrolled mirth, rolling on the ground. And so did a large number of the throng for there was no shortage of Celts in Rome, visiting satraps from Gaul and Germania, courtiers, men-at-arms, freed slaves, renegades, army auxiliaries, both foot and cavalry, and merchants and visitors.

It had to be explained to the puzzled warrior that it was Celtic allegory that had led to his public humiliation. The Hawthorn Queen and the Heron King were not enemy gods but merely the servant's colourful way of warning him to be on his guard against ripped breeches and of sinking deep in swamp mud.

It is not difficult to understand how the misunderstanding arose. Herons and hawthorn were just the kind of gods that the Britons did have in plenty, a pantheon of deities more like Kew Gardens and the Zoo rolled into one. In this blackthorn or may did play a part as well as oak and hazel. And the crane, a close enough relative of the heron that the Celts did not differentiate between them, was a bird of ill omen that brought misfortune to those who killed or trapped it. That the Roman was claiming that he had captured one added to the fun. He should have stuck to ducks, dogs, swans, ravens, jays, wild boar, and oxen – all bringers of good luck.

It must not be supposed that these vast number of species were sacrosanct like Hindu cattle. They ended up in the pot the same as the rest. But they were loved all the same, venerated for their importance to the tribal economy, just as the owner of a shoot fusses over his pheasants so he can kill them when the frosts roll round.

Clay or metal effigies of these hallowed beasts mounted on miniature ceremonial chariots were a common feature of Iron Age burials. Sacred animals also had human counterparts. The goddess Epona could at will assume the form of a horse and the famous stylised White Horse at Uffington, Berkshire, is thought to be she. It has been suggested that instead it should be called the White Cat of Uffington. It certainly looks more feline than equine.

There is also a strong feline flavour to this fifteen century roof boss in St Mary's church, Astbury, Cheshire.

The Romans were completely fascinated by the new island colony of Britain and the observations of visiting soldiers and administrators give tantalizing glimpses into the lives and beliefs of their new if unwilling subjects, often misinformed,

Cartmel Priory, Lancashire – an uncompromising three headed carving, note the three noses, on a mid fourteenth century misericord.

often misunderstood and always highly coloured. And they cannot help those little literary squeals of surprise and horror, just like prim Victorian missionaries when they described meeting the Hottentots of darkest Africa. There is also a wealth of information in the manuscripts of the early Irish monastic scribes which by chance escaped Christian vigilance, if only partially.

Three was a lucky number. Celtic bards grouped stories in threes called 'triads' and warriors fought in teams of three – spearman, shield-bearer and charioteer. Small wonder then that their gods came in trios, either as a composite of three deities or with three different names or identities.

Some high ranking male gods appear to be singular but even the chief god, Ar Dagda, meaning the 'good god', has two other names and the next senior, Lugh the Sun God, has other sneaky identities. The Celts bent or broke rules with impunity.

The mother goddess of war was three goddesses – Morrigan, Macha,

Cernunnos. the great antlered hunting god of the Celts, depicted on the silver Gundestrup Cauldron in the Danish National Museum in Copenhagen

and Bodh – but known collectively as Morrigna. Brigit, a close rival for supremacy and one whom the Christians made off with as Saint Bride, patron of those of literary bent, always appears as three images. And the Great Earth Mother herself is Agned, Annu, or Ann, Christianised as Saint Anne, grandmother of Jesus Christ, although she gets not a mention in the scriptures.

Male gods sometimes had female counterparts, strong evidence that the Celts of old – and new ones too – can always find a problem for every solution. Probably the white-robed postulants drummed up extra confusion so they could display their much vaunted skills of memory but a reasonably reliable rule of thumb is that female deities are all in some individual way representative of the ubiquitous earth mother goddess whereas the male gods seem occupied with the welfare of the tribe. In over-simplistic terms they are gods with appeal to members of the Women's Institute or those attracted to the Royal British Legion.

The names of a bewildering number of deities appear inscribed on effigies or occur in legends, poems or ancient manuscripts. In excess of four hundred have been listed but three-quarters of them occur only once so it is likely that a large number are local variants of pan-tribal supergods.

The classical historians seldom discuss them in detail and when they do they unhelpfully call them after the nearest Roman equivalent. The Greek poet Lucan, who wandered about Gaul in the second century AD thinking beautiful thoughts, did name three native gods – Esus, Taranis, and Tuatates – but he left no clue as to their function, although Taranis does mean 'thunder'.

There was a fundamental difference between the gods of the Celts and those of their Roman conquerors. Roman gods had human strengths and weaknesses and a citizen might mistake immortal for mortal, engage him or her in conversation, indulge in a love affair even. Celtic gods were often animals, as has been stated. If not they were supernatural – a collection of ghosts with ill defined genealogies and disordered personalities. A chat with one of these might leave one blind, hunchbacked or dead.

The gods were a tribe rather like an earthly one. At its head was Ar Dagda with his consort, the earth mother. Next in rank, just as in life, were the craftsmen-gods, blacksmiths, herbalists, healers, bards and harp-singers. It was a good thing to keep of the good side of Lugh for he may even be Ar Dagda in another guise. He wields enormous power and is of great significance as evidenced by elements of his name that survive in place names. He is also commemorated in the great end of summer festival, Lughnasadh, which was held on 1 August. This would make him a strong candidate for one of the identities from whom the Green Man is drawn if there were not an even stronger one – Cernunnos.

Antler horned Cernunnos – Saint Cornely to Christians, an imaginary pope martyred in 253 AD – is the lord of the hunt and numerous discoveries of antlered masks as grave goods suggest his following was widespread. The most famous representation of him is on a silver cauldron of the first century AD which had an interesting life of its own. It was stolen in antiquity from Gaul by Scandinavian seafarers and recovered at the end of the last century from a Danish bog where it may have been thrown to foil robbers.

Or it may have been a votive offering to the water dragon or serpent living in the bog and known as the 'nicor'. Beowulf's mortal enemy Grendel was a 'nicor' and so was Grendel's mother. One still lives in a pool at

Folk memory of the ancient skull cult or eighteenth century taste for the macabre? This Death's Head Green Man is at the base of the Sandford and Challoner memorial at St Mary Redcliffe church, Bristol.

Lyminster in West Sussex in what is called the Knucker Hole – not a bad rendition of the old Saxon name after a thousand years.

One might write a book about the cauldron and its *repousse* figures. Cernunnos sits in majesty, a torque about his neck and holding another in his right hand, powerful symbols of good fortune. Because of his horns the Christians were quick to identify him as the Devil himself. As Lord of the Forest as well he has excellent qualifications for the role of archetypal Green Man.

Herne the Hunter – also Cernunnos in another guise – is, like Robin Hood, deeply entrenched in folklore. Bearded, mighty, and riding a black horse he hunts with a pack of fierce hounds across the sky on stormy nights. He is said to haunt Windsor Great Park and the local paper reports without a smile that a large number of 'reliable' witnesses saw him when he last appeared in 1962.

And there is the even more terrifying and widespread cult of the human head without which any account of Celtic gods or the Green Man would be incomplete .

Diodorus Siculus writes:

They cut off the heads of enemies slain in battle and attach them to the necks of their horses. These blood-stained spoils they hand over to their attendants to carry them away as booty while striking up a paean and singing a song of victory. And they nail them up on their houses. They also embalm in cedar oil the heads of the most distinguished enemies and preserve them carefully in a chest and display them with pride to strangers saying for this head or that one of their ancestors, or his father, or the man himself refused the offer of a large sum of money. Some of them boast that they have refused the weight of the head in gold.

Livy supports his deeply disturbed countryman:

The [Roman] Consuls got no report of the disaster until some Gallic horse-men came in sight with heads hanging at their horses' breasts or fixed on their lances and singing their customary songs of triumph.

He adds that they cleansed the skulls of their more important victims and after mounting with gold use them as holy vessels for libations to their gods or they became drinking vessels for priests and temple attendants. By this magic the tribesmen assumed the power of their vanquished foes, and the higher the rank the better.

The skulls were nailed to gates to protect the community from evil and they are often found during excavations of sites such as farm buildings which have no special ritual association. At Danbury, Essex skulls were found at the bottom of Iron Age grain storage pits to assure future good harvests.

Romans apart, the most reliable evidence for the cult of the severed head is at Roquepertuis, north of Aix-en-Provence in southern France where three columns of a portal of possibly the first century BC were uncovered. Each of the columns had been decorated with paintings of fish and importantly for our quest – foliage. And each had recesses for human skulls, some of which were still in place.

Not far away, at Entremont, a tall pillar carved with twelve human heads was unearthed together with a large number of sculpted heads of men, women and children. Nearby was a fearsome stone monster in the process of devouring a stone human corpse. Clenched in its claws were stone human heads.

It is from this cult of human heads that a distinctive form of early Celtic ecclesiastical art derives. Thus it is logical to claim that the stone heads that decorate the Romanesque doorways at Dysert O'Dea and at Clonfert, both in Ireland, are survivals of a tradition that once pertained throughout the whole of Britain and they differ little from those at the pagan shrine at Entremont. Or, pursuing the theme further, is there much difference between the Irish heads and the leaf surrounded heads with branches clenched between their jaws of two or three centuries later.

This puts our Green Man in a direct line that stretches back to the cult heads of that part of ancient time we have come to call Prehistory. He was undoubtedly pre-Christian in conception but used later by Christians fearful of the Old Religion.

To be bolder the medieval Green Man of the churches and the modernish Green Man that dances round the maypole as Jack in the Green is in fact the Old Man of the Trees, as the monk chroniclers sometimes called him, a Druid seen through the eyes of Christianity.

4

WHERE TO LOOK

THE survival of early Green Men is often due to luck and seldom to judgement. It would be nice to think of the local parish church as a rock standing firm in the fierce tides of history, whereas a storm tossed pebble might be a more accurate analogy. What we see today, and it would be unnatural if it were otherwise, is the result of a thousand years of meddling, of the whims and passions of crowned and mitred heads, doctrinal and liturgical schisms and changes, and benefactors 'doing things' so that they might be remembered.

With all these debilitating forces at work it is a wonder that our 17,000 underfunded parish churches are as beautiful and well preserved as they are. For in England exists the quixotic situation of an Established Church whose buildings are neither the property nor the responsibility of the State.

Those relentless progressives, the Victorians, with their new mass-produced materials, did the the most damage. Priceless medieval stained glass was replaced with a painted variety which made dark church interiors even darker. The gloom may have lent heels to their equally destructive passion for covering medieval wall paintings with whitewash and varnishing old stonework to make it shine. They tore up ancient floors to lay shiny tiles and pulpits and benches were made to glitter like the quarterdecks of dreadnoughts with brasswork. New fangled guttering and drainpipes certainly put paid to gargoyles and exterior ornaments although it must be said that gargoyles had long been out of fashion although there were some eccentric revivals.

The glory of a French church interior is its sculpture and stained glass; for Italy it is sculpture and paintings; for the British Isles it is its woodwork. The three major items of parish church woodwork are screens, stalls

Green Men on misericords – in Holy Trinity church, Coventry and, below, in St Katherine's, Loversall, Yorkshire.

and roofs – all fine Green Man hunting country.

The function of the screen, apart from supporting a cross and sometimes a loft, was to protect the chancel and the altar from the curious eyes of laymen and to close off the nave so that it could be used for more earthly parish functions. It is is one of the more obscure traditions, even a legal obligation, that beyond the screen the care of the church resides with the rector while the rest is paid for by the parishioners.

The best screens are to be found in East Anglia or the south-west. As far as the Middle Ages are concerned Norfolk and Suffolk were by far the richer, the churches larger and loftier, but screens anywhere were originally a blaze of colour, the panels usually filled with the apostles and saints.

Sometimes the artist breaks free from tradition and the most unlikely figures occur. One painting in St Gregory's, Sudbury, Suffolk, depicts a physician curing gout by conjuring a demon out of his patient's boot.

There are imps, demons, animals to be seen – and all too rarely the Green Man –

but it is always worth taking a look.

The taste for sermonising, which reached a peak at the end of the thirteenth century, and the provision of stalls for those who were obliged to stand and listen to them – lay and otherwise – cannot be entirely unconnected. Even so the humbler classes were made to stand until the end of the fifteenth century. That cheerful despot Henry V111 helped the cause if unwittingly by his mass closure of religious foundations which flooded the market with surplus ecclesiastical furniture. On bench-ends and stalls, canopied or otherwise, Green Men abound.

Another favourite place is the misericord, a piece of ecclesiastical duplicity. It is a corbel-like wooden bracket under a tip-up seat on which monks and clergy might perch while to all outwards appearances standing. Because misericords were mostly out of sight they allowed the carver full scope to indulge his fantasies and they are among the finer contributions to the beauty of our churches. They are also prime hunting grounds for Green Men, particularly if the stalls came from monastic or collegiate foundations as a result of King Hal's furniture sale.

Several thousand misericords survive, mainly of the fourteenth and fifteenth centuries. As one might expect the best are in cathedrals and considered to be masterpieces in craftsmanship and design; the worst are clumsy and crude but even these have charm. All tell about medieval life, costumes and customs and even sports and games.

Some of the most beautiful timber roofs in the world are found in English parish churches and it is not surprising that carpenters were rated second only to to masons in the hierarchy of the medieval building business. Wood carvers were similarly celebrated and some of the finest, and most frightening, Green Men are found in abundance as roof bosses where timbers cross or meet.

Masonry Green Men can be found as corbels, tombs, friezes, capitals, pillars, tympana, door jambs, spandrels, lintels and roundels. In woodwork he occurs in many forms – as a leaf with human features, as a cluster of leaves with human features, as a leaf mask, as a human head looking through foliage like someone after a lost cricket ball in an unfriendly neighbour's garden, and as a human head disgorging or perhaps swallowing leafy branches which emanate from his mouth, his eyes and sometimes nose as well. He has appeared as a hybrid of all these styles. The ages pass and he erupts, flourishes, dies, only to be reborn generations later.

Devilish Green Men, tongues out against authority, on a roof boss in St Mary's church, South Tawton, Devon and, below, as part of a wall carving in St Teilo's church, Llantilio Crossenney, Monmouthshire (Gwent).

Examples of frightening and extremely foliate early fourteenth century roof
bosses in Exeter Cathedral

That the choice of Green Men as church decoration was fortuitous and resulted from the limited repertoire of rustic wood-carvers seems unlikely for he occurs all over Western Europe, wherever Christianity pertains. Like old enemies they seem to be mutually attracted, inseparable. This bizarre association poses the tricky question of what the representation of a pagan god is doing in the temples of a religion dedicated to his destruction and for which he was the incarnation of evil.

The quaint habit of early Christians in transforming troublesome pagan gods into 'saints' might provide at least some of the answer if not all of it. He seems to have been an unwelcome guest for far from calling him a saint and fitting him out with a few miracles the Church maintains an impenetrable silence about him. Sometimes he is even fashioned with unpleasant facial expressions, often with his tongue out, not only the reaction of rude little boys to authority but a characteristic of the Devil himself.

One might ponder his role in the pantheon of Druidical gods but it must have been an earthy one and he was popular with common folk judging by his numerous appearances in various guises at festivals, fairs and other jolly occasions. He is the Summer Lord. On May Day he is crowned king. He arrives garlanded or concealed in shrubbery to cheers and raised mugs of ale. He romps around the maypole and joins the Morris dancers as Jack in the Green or Robin Hood.

Perhaps closer still to the Green Man of old was the itinerant pedlar of herbal remedies for all ills, usually encountered at country fairs and festivals until the turn of the century. He wore clothing stitched with leaves and a tall hat bedecked with leafy fronds, even dying his face green. Quack or magician? Nobody cared if the cure worked. And he soon made himself scarce if it did not.

But why did simple folk love the Green Man and the Church not at all? We must take a leap in the dark. His rebirth seems to coincide with some major human disaster and there was a great eruption of Green Men as result of that most terrible century of a terrible age.

Well before the fourteen century things were going badly wrong. There was interminable strife between rival feudal lords and between them and the king and vast tracts of the countryside were laid waste by civil war. There was already a serious food shortage and humble people starved but then came a succession of rainless winters and tropical summers followed by the most terrible scourge of all – the Black Death. This series of plagues wiped out two thirds of the inhabitants of England and the Continent. It was truly an affliction of Old Testament proportions and the common man must have thought that God had forsaken him - if He had ever cared.

Christianity was elitist and unconcerned with the lives of common folk. It seemed to glorify in suffering and death. It venerated the crucifixion of Jesus Christ and the agony of other saintly martyrs down the ages. It dwelt on the heat of Hell and a freezing Purgatory, the living death for sinners and poverty was a sin. With death all around them and the religion of the Virgin and Child seemingly indifferent to their plight, the people began to look elsewhere for deliverance.

Surviving in folk memory was the Old Religion whose quintessence was Life. It rejoiced in natural things, the spirits of wind, earth, water, of vegetation. Even its temples, the sacred oak groves, had been in the open-air. None may have remembered white-robed priests who cut mistletoe with golden sickles, stood on one leg, closed an eye and pointed to cast spells and predict the future but there was a folk culture of omens, portents, charms, witches, fairies and things that went bump in the night and how passing under a ladder brought bad luck and that sprinkling salt over the left shoulder with the right hand averted it.

To this belief belonged the Green Man. The Church, fearing it was losing credibility fought back with one of its old conversions. It allowed the evil spirit to enter by the back-door in the form of decoration. Only by this compromise might he be tamed.

All this is surmise. We cannot be sure that the Green Man was a pre-Christian god and a very powerful one although folk memory or tradition tells us that he was and that he personified the annual death and rebirth of the earth and was Lord of the Greenwood. There is more than a good chance that his voice is the roar of beech in a gale, the hiss of ash in a high wind, the breathless hush of a winter forest and the tumult of woodland in spring.

When we hear him no more, he - and life - will be at an end.

Carvings on capitals – at Beverley Minster and, below, Lichfield Cathedral where, in 1340, an English underdog works off a grudge with a *tete de feuilles* with more than a passing resemblance to the king's master mason.

5

THE FOLKLORE OF ENGLAND AND THE GREEN MAN

LEGENDS, myths, fables, even fairy tales were the ways in which a non-literate society told its story. Distorted, emphasis changed to suit the talker's purpose maybe, but here is real history told in a shy or obscure way. This is perhaps the greatest discovery by archaeologists in the last fifty years.

For some this claim is too ambitious but that fact is often disguised as myth is demonstrated in the antique collection of Welsh tales which were discovered last century and thought to be nursery tales for medieval children. The collection is called *Mabinogion*

The passion of Prince Culhwch – pronounced Kilhooch with a throat clearing on the 'ch' – for Olwen, daughter of the giant Ysbaddaden, need not concern us but the prince's allies in achieving his amorous goal include not only hobgoblins with fantastic powers but two historical characters plus a third whose existence is thought to be likely, or not impossible.

The uncertain one is the best known – King Arthur – but there is no doubt about Saint Gildas, the monk-historian who wrote a short work moaning about tardy British military leaders who fiddled and worse while Britain was put to the fire and the sword by Saxon invaders. Or Taliesin, bard, poet and probably Druid. Both lived in the early part of the sixth century. As an example of the power of folk memory, Culhwch and Olwen, not written down until the twelfth century, cannot be rivalled.

It is from similar material that our Green Man is likely to emerge. Some of the tales make little sense other than they seem to be telling a forbidden

The twelfth century doorway of the Church of St Mary and St David at Kilpeck,
Herefordshire, is one of the most precious architectural treasures in England.
The central motif is the Tree of Life and, as well as Green Men – there is one on
top of the righthand door pillar, another on the garland above the door –it
depicts a variety of creatures

or elusive story. All the stories below are whispers from other times to aid us in our hunt for the origins of the Green Man.

It would be as well to emphasise that while the English think of themselves as Anglo-Saxons they do so without real justification. When the Anglo-Saxons landed in these islands the native population was much the same as it was when the Romans arrived three hundred years before. It was a collection of Celtic tribes, with the Cymri, an older race than the Celts, to the far west in what is now Wales and the Scotii and Picti in the far north.

Despite the sixth century ranting of old Gildas the Wise and the solemn pronouncements of Victorian historians in the nineteenth archaeologists have found little evidence in the form of charred ruins and mass graves to support the view that towns and villages were torched and populations butchered or forced to migrate. Almost unexceptionally the digs suggest continuity, with life ambling on in its uneventful way, and the Celts staying put and intermarrying with the new settlers. Thus the blood that flows through the veins of the major part of the so called Anglo-Saxons is Anglo-Celtic or if one, prefers Saxon-Celtic. This allows the present author the luxury of the short term 'Celt' for them all.

ANIMAL MAGIC

Hares

SOME countrymen refuse to eat the hare rather than risk cannibalism. Sacred to the Celts, consequently the hare is a witch in disguise for Christians. In this disguise they range far and wide, causing mischief, overhearing secrets, helping themselves to milk from cows. Immortal except to a silver bullet extreme bad luck will follow if one crosses your path. Return home and try again tomorrow.

Boudicca, Queen of the Iceni set a hare free, watched the way it fled and saw it augured well for a successful outcome of her rebellion against the might of Rome. So says one classical historian but he omitted to mention that the mighty Warrior Queen's army was defeated and she killed herself by poison. Perhaps that particular hare was an under-cover agent for the Romans.

Shrews

IN southern England these little creatures were once known as 'over-runners' which is reckoned to be a memory of the old tradition that one running over a foot was mighty unlucky. One running over a cow caused its milk to dry up.

Snakes

THE inbuilt loathing that so many people have for reptiles made it inevitable that the early Christians claimed that Druids hatched from snake eggs. The tradition that St Patrick charmed the entire population of snakes out of Ireland assumes a new dimension in this context.

It is authoritively claimed, by biased Romans, that the Druids had a thriving serpent cult and the Feast of Imbolc (February 1) later the Christian Feast of St Bridget or St Bride, was 'the day of the serpent' although it is too early in the year for the reptiles to participate themselves.

Famous too are 'serpent stones' or serpents said to have been turned into stone by kindly intervention of saintly monks. They are usually anything that looks the part – odd shaped lumps of rock, glass beads, even fossil ammonites, a large snail that once populated the oceans.

Snails

IT is said that an old name for the snail is 'dodman' or 'deadman' and some believe this derives not from 'dead' in the sense of lifeless but that used by sea navigators as in 'dead reckoning'. Behind this assertion are the two 'poles' or antenna on the snail's head, said to be like the twin poles carried by the village 'dodman' of yore who measured field boundaries and adjudicated in disputes over property rights.

Regarded as positive proof that the 'dodman' actually existed is the giant hill figure at Wilmington in East Sussex who is actually carrying the poles like a badge of office. A small hole in this otherwise excellent theory is that there is not a single mention of this rustic official in any historical document relating to property. Another quibble is that the term 'dead reckoning' is comparatively modern and comes not from 'dead' but 'ded', short for 'deduced reckoning.'

The assertion that the giant may have been called 'The Green Man of Wilmington' at one time adds heat to the dispute. But it does seem more probable the 'dodman' did in fact get his name as a result of his deadly slow mode of progress. In some parts treated as a lucky charm he should be tossed over the head while reciting:

Lucky snail, go over my head
And bring me a penny before I go to bed

The Cornish regard snails as bearers of bad tidings. A tin miner who encounters a snail on his way to work must offer it a placatory crumb of food or fragment of candle. To be overtaken by one on the way to the mine was more ominous.

THE CHRISTIAN AND CELTIC CALENDARS

Candlemas Day (February 2)

THIS takes its name from the candles that were distributed and carried in church processions of the festival that conveniently coincides with the old bonfire festival of Imbolc.

There is more than a hint of its connection with St Bride or Bridget, thought to be the daughter, even consort, of the chief Celtic god, Ar Dagda. In the Christian context she is given the role of midwife to the birth of Jesus and like his grandmother, Anne, was introduced later and is not a biblical chracater.

Corn dollies fashioned at harvest were ceremonially borne to the fields at Candlemas and ploughed in to return the spirit to the earth.

Exeter Cathedral corbel with luxuriant vegetation flowing from a Green Man to glorify the Blessed Virgin and Child.

51

Imbolc

IMBOLC is a 'quarter of the year' day of the Old Religion and corresponds to February 1. The other quarter days are Beltane (May 1), Lughnasadh (August 1) and Samhain (November 1), which is the start of the Celtic year.

May Day

BELTANE in the old Celtic calender was the most potent festival for the Green Man and for vegetation, for wild creatures, for poets, agriculturalists and lovers alike. Some folk even see the Maypole as a phallic symbol but some see phallic symbols in wine or sauce bottles.

Jack in the Green heads a 1937 May Day procession at Pulborough, West Sussex.

In times of the Druids the bonfires were enormous, significance forgotten, but fire was said to consume evil spirits or perhaps they were just warm and interesting to stand around. There is something uncanny about the way people continue to look into a barbecue even when the last burnt sausage has been consumed.

It is the festival of the Green Man – as himself, as Jack in the Green, Robin Goodfellow, Robin Hood. And his consort called Maid Marian or more prissily the May Queen. Sometimes he is even a chimney sweep or someone dressed to resemble one. The Church is accused of intruding this sombre figure into the jollity as a reminder of the devil and wicked associations. However, dark figures are not always symbolic of death but rather good fortune or luck as in the welcome given to dark people who cross the threshold after midnight on the last day of the year.

May Day is also called Garland Day, possibly a later and more youthful festival and divorced from the more robust beer and skittles of the adults. Children paraded with bunches of spring flowers and dolls called 'May babies' in arms or white boxes, always covered. 'Would you like to see my May baby?' the tiny tots asked and the gift a halfpenny was most times-forthcoming. 'A penny for the guy?' may have its origins here. Or perhaps the hunger that was all too common among humble folk.

St Bartholemew's Day (August 24)

AS this good saint is patron of bee-keepers there are no prizes for guessing that this is the old Celtic Festival of the Bee for which these valuable insects were tribal gods. There is a tradition that bees must be told of a death in the family and this suggests that in addition to the benison of honey they were the messengers of the Otherworld .

At Witton in Yorkshire an enormous straw image known as the the Bartle – possibly a corruption of the saint's name – is carried in procession to a bonfire where it is burnt. He is believed to be a harvest god and thus has an affinity with the Green Man.

St Bridget's Day (July 23)

SHE was a powerful triple goddess of the Old Religion, commemorated in modern times as a not quite top ranking patron saint of arts and crafts. Significant is that she has many wells dedicated to her throughout the country. In the old days the major part of northern Britain was occupied by a a powerful Celtic tribe named for her, the Brigantes. She is the only Christian saint who has two days on which she is venerated. The other is February 2.

ANCIENT CUSTOMS AND CHARACTERS

Clipping the Church

THE parishioners link hands on Saint Bride's Day, February 1 and walk or dance clockwise or 'the way of the sun' around the church singing, often to the accompaniment of the town band.

The date may be significant for it is the old Celtic feast of Imbolc when ritual dances at prehistoric stones were the custom and there is the view that Christians built their early churches on pagan sites. More meaty, perhaps, is the oft repeated legend that this or that prehistoric circle was formed of revellers changed into stone for dancing on Sunday, a none too subtle hint from the Church that dancing there at all was evil.

Chanctonbury Ring, the famous clump of beech trees above Wiston, West Sussex, has a similar tradition. To conjure up the Devil you run around it backwards three times in an anti-clockwise direction – a next to impossible feat due to the vast size of the ring and the precipitous terrain.

Harvest

IMBOLC, February 1, saw the ploughing in of the corn dolly made at the feast of Lughnasadh. In some parts of the country a whole sheaf of corn was buried. As the reapers approached the last stand it was traditional for them to look the other way or to cover their faces.

This custom or 'courtesy', was to conceal the identity the reaper who cut the final swathe. Hard to explain is why in some areas the final passage with scythe or sickle is called 'cutting the neck' or 'crying the mare'.

Hobby horses

THE hobby horse is the most popular and feared member of a morris-dancing side. Probably the best known is the 'Oss of Padstow although his hoop shape and fearsome head bears no resemblance to the horse in nature. The morris figure is more orthodox. This give rise to conjecture that the original figure was not a horse at all but a mythical creature, perhaps a dragon.

This odd transformation into a dragon is repeated at other traditional festivals, for example the famous Snap the Dragon at Norwich. Various frightful beasts also appear in other parts of the West Country and in the Cotswolds and Kent.

Some authorities are still prepared to accept that the hobby horses are associated with Epona the horse god. It is also possible that down the years they have changed into frighteners to put parishioners off Druidism or witchcraft, which the Old Religion was often called.

Morris Dancing

THIS highly-popular spectacle is most often performed in pub forecourts on and after May Day and used to include mummers who performed simple folk plays.

Nowadays it is almost always reduced to the dancers who, according to whim, may include Robin Hood, Maid Marian – originally portrayed by a man – and Jack in the Green who is always explained in the literature as the Spirit of the Greenwood or the Green Man.

Other characters are Friar Tuck, and the Fool or Jester who lays about him with an inflated pig's bladder. In earlier times Robin and Marian were the Lord and Lady, even King and Queen. The drink and drive laws have taken the fun out of the performances and the Round Hill side from Steyning, Sussex is inclined to temperance, or thinking about it.

Ooser

THIS figure was common to every Dorset village but the ooser – a horned mask with staring eyes and bared teeth – was also known elsewhere in rural England. He capered in processions at village fetes and festivals and made mock attacks on the crowd, which obligingly ran away screaming. With some, particularly women and young children, the screams were genuine.

During the night preceding May Day a maypole was set up in the Frying Pan, an earthwork just above the famous Cerne Abbas Giant. At dawn the maypole was decked with flowers and the dance began, the ooser joining in. The last ooser ritual was conducted at Melbury Osmond at the beginning of this century although with the current folk dancing revival he is making a comeback.

The ooser may be a manifestation of Cernunnus but horns not antlers suggest a deity more appropriate to cattle rather than the chase. Whatever god he was his name has not come down to us and his belligerent attentions suggest human sacrifice or Christian scare tactics.

Well-dressing

THE reverence of the Druids for pools and springs suggests that the ceremony of well-dressing on Ascension Day is another Christian take-over.

Horror heads of Green Men on roof bosses in St Andrew's church, South Tawton and, below, another at St Andrew's, Sampford Courtenay. They date from the fourteenth or the fifteenth century.

The dressing, where the custom still survives, is usually in the form of flower petals pressed into wet clay to illustrate a biblical story. That clergy are in attendance to bless the well attests to the still potent magic of the Old Religion.

LEGENDS ABOUT PEOPLE AND PLACES

Black Annis

THIS is one of the oldest and most obscure legends of the British Isles. Black Annis was an old woman who lived on a desolate heath near where Leicester stands today. She is described variously as witch, ogre, or monster and all agree that she ate children.

The name has also been rendered as Annu, the earth mother and wife of Lugh, the sun god, both considered benevolent deities 'but', adds one account savagely, 'their worship did include the sacrifice of children at certain festivals.' No prizes for guessing that the author was a parson.

Bradford Head Cult

THE Great Crop Circle Mystery has a parallel with the discovery of grotesque stone heads built into the masonry of farmsteads, cottages and field walls. Archaeologists are of the opinion that they have strong affinities with Celtic head carvings of almost two millennia ago, the cult that succeeded the collection of real human heads.

Stonework in isolation is difficult to date and although from archaeological considerations some of the heads seem to be genuine others are thought to be recent, no more than a hundred years old, with the implication that either the Celtic head cult survived into the time of Queen Victoria or they are another student tease.

In the context of a hoax one cannot ignore the weakness in the North – or is it a strength? – for 'gurning', that is the pulling of funny faces by those with no need to bother.

Burrey Man

THIS folklore figure, once nationwide but now confined to Queensferry, West Lothian, could almost pass for the Green Man except his appearance is connected solely with the harvest, the old Celtic festival of Lughnasadh.

The Burrey Man parades through the town and is pelted with sticky burrs, hence his name, which are said to represent the sins of the village. At at the end of the parade he is ritually expelled. One strongly suspects that this meaningless but enjoyable frolic once had deep significance.

Leys

A FASCINATING hypothesis with an enormous number of enthusiastic followers was arrived at one summer's day in 1920 when 'in one instant flash of recognition' Alfred Watkins saw stretching away into the misty distance church steeples, standing stones, earth mounds and moats linked by dead straight trackways.

Another curious feature was that where old paths crossed the skyline they were marked by natural notches or mounds beckoning the traveller on. Watkins believed he had discovered a system of ancient ' sighting-pegs' by which our prehistoric ancestors found their way around. He called the alignments 'leys' from the Old English 'lea' which meant a tract of open ground. He thought the word apt although his reasoning is obscure. Watkins was prone to nagging arguments. His *Early British Trackways* and its extension and modern ley hunter's bible, *The Old Straight Track,* were attempts to answer criticism before it came.

Academic historians are notoriously resistant to breathtaking and revolutionary theories, particularly those of amateurs which threaten to grab orthodoxy by the collar and give it a good shake. The chorus of condemnation from Oxbridge was loud and scathing, some of it hinting that the author's connection with the brewing trade might be a causative factor.

The connection was brief. From several generations of farmers his father had moved in 1920 into business as miller, corn-dealer and brewer. It was only natural that on leaving school young Watkins became his father's representative but he was soon in business in his own right as the inventor and seller of a highly successful photographic exposure meter which sold in hundreds of thousands throughout the world. He was a keen photographer and also interested in archaeology and he loved the countryside, its legends and customs.

The first of many objections to Watkins's leys was the ragbag of sites that formed them. He included earth barrows and churches in his align-

The kind of expression of optimism and catastrophe one sees in the faces of down-and-outs is worn by this Green Man in St Mary Redcliffe, Bristol.

ment although they were not contemporaneous and therefore not available to his fantasy prehistoric route-maker.

Watkins argued continuence. Churches were usually built on pre-Christian sites – Avebury, for instance, actually had a church inside its ring of stones – so that resolved that argument. Among other issues was the small number of ancient sites required for a Watkins ley – three was not really enough for two would naturally fall into alignment and only a coincidental third was required to qualify. One wag said that any number of leys could be imagined with Watneys pubs in London.

But if the majority of academic historians remain sceptical a small number do think that the Watkins hypothesis might have foundation. Ancient sites do have an uncanny knack of falling into line. While walking from the Devon to The Wash to establish whether there was an ancient long distance route across Britain the author could not help but notice the number of times Bronze Age barrows and Iron Age hill forts that did appear to form leys. His reservation is that these sites are so numerous that they cannot help but fall into line.

Watkins has a vast numbers of followers throughout the western world. All one needs is a large scale Ordnance Survey map, a ruler and a pencil. And, of course, a pair of walking shoes for half the fun is following in the footsteps of the ancient route-masters of long ago.

Robin Hood

THE presence of an elusive and mysterious character in the greenwood invites identification with woodland spirits or gods and, of course, the Green Man. He is also called Robin Goodfellow, Jack in the Green, King of the Garland and Puck and is god of the forest under another name. His consort is Maid Marian and together they play the part of king and queen in May Day and Midsummer's Day frolics.

Robin Hood has been transferred fictionally to the Forest of Sherwood but he was once widespread and on the borders of Herefordshire, possibly the limit of his range, he become synonymous with the Devil and the Wild Hunt. Is it significant that there are more pubs in London named the Green Man than there are in Nottinghamshire?

Stonehenge

THERE are more theories about this ancient monument than all the rest put together, not the least being how the stones arrived and how they were erected. According to legend the Devil brought the stones from Ireland and sneaked them up one dark night. The stealth was in vain for he was seen by a friar and was so startled that he dropped the final stone in near-by Bulford Brook where it lies today. He threw another after the fleeing friar which struck him on the heel thus leaving a mark and giving one of the monoliths its name – Heel Stone. The name, in fact, comes from the Old Celtic 'hel' which means 'sun'.

The story that the stones came from Ireland was probably lifted from Geoffrey of Monmouth, purveyor of Arthurian fables to Henry II, a king who succeeded in persuading himself that he was a direct descendant of Arthur.

Geoffrey says the stones came from an Irish mountain called Killaurus and were transported in distant times from the furthest ends of Africa and set up in a circle. Many expeditions across the Irish Sea failed to shift them until Merlin the Wizard built several 'engines' which were successful: 'laid them down so light that none would believe, and bade them [presumably his helpers] carry them to the ships.'

The fact that the 'blue' stones came from the Prescelly Mountains in what used to be called Pembrokeshire ruins a good yarn and its use of Geoffrey's medieval material suggests that it was a later Christian parable of the Right versus Wrong genre.

William Rufus

THERE is a persistent myth that the hunting accident that overtook William Rufus in the summer of 1100 in the New Forest was ritual slaughter and that he was sacrificed to appease the spirits of the Greenwood or even the Green Man himself.

The red-haired king was not the first in the family to die that year. His nephew, the illegitimate son of his brother Robert, had been slain in May but his illegitimacy was thought to have robbed the sacrifice of potency. Another was required, this time of the king himself and on a more important festival, Lugnasadh at the beginning of August.

It was the circumstances of the deaths, meaningless unless symbolic of something deeper, that attracted attention, particularly from those prone to conspiracy theories. Both were said to have been slain by silver arrows in a sacred grove, the king under an oak while the bowman stood under an alder, both sacred to tree worshippers of old, and according to one account both were victims of the same archer. That the king's blood reportedly dripped on the ground as he was borne to Romsey Abbey sounds like some pagan ritual, particularly as modern medical authorities say it is extremely unlikely for this to happen after death – and impossible after an arrow strike.

Little more needs to be said except that Lugnasadh is less auspicious as a killing day than May Day. Witchcraft or no it is a fact that young brother Henry did leave the forest in suspicious haste in order, it was claimed, to secure the crown and the royal treasure, not bothering one whit about the dead king. This makes it likely but by no means certain that both William and Robert met their deaths through pre-arranged accident, not an unprecedented occurrence in medieval society.

PLANT LORE

Ferns

THE barely visible seeds of ferns confer invisibility if gathered by shaking them on to a pewter plate at midnight on Midsummer's Eve. The Devil regards invisibility as disrespectful and will send wind and rain and play other diabolic tricks to thwart would-be gatherers – that is if the Devil needs to intervene in this almost impossible task.

Some must have had some managed it however for if a young woman runs three times around a church while the bell strikes midnight sowing fern seeds as she goes she will see her future husband scything down the bed of fern from whence the seeds were gathered.

Groundsel

GROUNDSEL is a good example of a plant dear to the Druids and bad news for Christians. It has associations with witches by the covens; a largish patch in a field is caused by a meeting of them; a small patch where one answered a call of nature. The Devil will invite into his presence individuals who carry a posy of it. This means that witches can die only from July to October. When worn it is a charm against the Evil Eye and witches.

Mistletoe

MOST sacred plant of all to the Druids thus the most anathematised by the Christians and forbidden entry to churches.

According to one classical historian the Druids believed the soul of the oak dwelt in the berry of the mistletoe and that its removal was a preliminary to the felling of the tree. This is incredible, inconceivable. Oaks were venerated, a tradition that travelled almost intact down the centuries to modern times. In many villages there is a memory if nothing more of the rural parliament that met under a venerable oak. The gnarled remains of one still stands in Amberly, West Sussex. Unknown to that particular Roman, mistletoe is rarely found growing on oaks. The most frequent hosts to this marvellous parasite are apple and poplar.

Norse mythology gives an entirely different view of *Viscum album* than that associated with Druidism. There is the saga of Baldur the Fair whose

A 'stretched' Green Man with a wide smile is carved on a lintel in Hereford
Cathedral.

fear of death drove him to ask the gods at the roots of Yggdrasil to per-
suade everything on earth to swear they would not harm him. Everything
agreed. Unfortunately the emissary of the gods Frigg left out mistletoe and
Loki the Evil provided Hodr, a blind god, with a dart of mistletoe with
fatal consequences for Baldur.

It seems strange therefore that there is an old tradition that a sprig of
mistletoe cut with a new knife on Hallowe'en after walking around the
tree prevented wounding in battle. This sounds like a mix-up of Druid and
Viking lore and unsafe.

St John's Wort

THAT it bloomed at midsummer assured a name change from 'amber' to
its present one to marry with the Christian takeover of the Midsummer
bonfire festival on St John's Eve. It has the usual anti-witch association
when bunches were hung over doors on Midsummer's Eve but another
strange belief is that one can look through a bunch of the flowers into the
flames of a bonfire without harming the eyes. It was so much in demand
for this charm it was believed to hide from would-be gatherers.

SOME MORE SUPERSTITIONS

Iron

It is not generally known that it was not the horse-shoe but the iron from
which it was forged that brought good luck. There is the view that fear of
iron is a survival from the Bronze Age, a leftover from the superiority of

iron weapons of the new invaders. And that is why the superior tribal god of the Celts, the great iron users, was a blacksmith. This being so it is surprising that some ingenious theorist has not advanced the same view about salt, for the Celts as a race received early impetus from the mining of the mineral. Why a pinch of spilt salt cast over the left shoulder averts bad luck is unclear.

Iron keeps away fairies and witches and a key or knife or any iron object placed under a chair occupied by a witch will render her (or him for a modern witch can be male or female) harmless.

Old shoes

CHILDREN'S shoes particularly, deliberately rendered unwearable, are often discovered in the fabric of old buildings. Folklore insists that these are good luck charms but is silent on the significance of youthful footwear. Grimmer accounts hint that it is a survival of child sacrifice. And it is recorded that human corpses were thrown into the mortar of new buildings although this was reckoned to be less of a sacred ritual than that human blood made mortar harder.

In more enlightened modern times there is the tradition of throwing old shoes after a departing newly-married couple for good luck.

TREES AND THEIR TRADITIONS

The apple

THE mysticism of the apple tree got it elected as the tree of Adam and Eve and the Garden of Eden and from here it was a small jump to lending its name to the Island of Apples – Avalon – to whence King Arthur was borne after his mortal wounding at the Battle of Camlann. This ignores the fact that the Celts of old had little truck with apples and believed that the spirits of the dead went to the Isle of the Winds or Avelou and thus suggests mistranslation.

It is unlucky to fell an apple tree and the odd spray of blossom persisting until the autumn when the apples are ripe is an indication of a death in the family. It has even argued, but on no reliable evidence, that the

Druidical ritual of cutting mistletoe has been translated from the apple to the oak. The ceremony was a winter one associated with wassailing the apple trees and the hunting of the wren or sometimes the robin, both regarded as the spirit of the apple tree.

The ash

POSSIBLY a case of a forgotten tradition but the ash seems to be an anathema to Celts while to the rest, particularly Saxons and Norsemen, it is regarded as the hub of the universe. The ash is Yggdrasil – the Earth Tree that upholds the heavens while its roots descend to hell where they are gnawed by serpents. Here is the Underworld where the gods meet in solemn conclave to decide our fate. They are kept in touch with earthly developments by an eagle and a squirrel who dwell in the branches of the ash.

The Yule Log burned from Christmas to the New Year was traditionally ash. A cure for rupture or hernia is an ash sapling with a split two or three feet long that allows the sufferer to pass through from east to west. After this the ends are bound together. It is imperative that there is dew on the ground during the course of the cure.

A live shrew buried in a plugged hole, thereafter called a 'shrew-ash', will discourage witches. It will certainly discourage shrews.

The birch

THE birch, which is short-lived and rots as it grows, is associated with May Day celebrations and in some parts of the country the maypole around which the dancers jig is made of birch. A few birch branches about a door scares away witches, a fact of which some witches are unaware for they happily fly through the sky on birch besoms. How this contradictory circumstance arose is bewildering but in times past people with no permanent lodging were wed if they linked hands and jumped over a besom and in some parts churched couples were not 'properly' married until they took the leap.

The bramble

ALTHOUGH more a bush than a tree the bramble or blackberry, was particularly venerated by the Celts and joins rowan and oak as a component of ritual pyres. Passing through a wild or natural arch of bramble eases whooping cough although for a cure the sufferer is required to hazard his skin on nine successive days. A small complication may arise through the insistence that the arch is on a parish boundary and the patient must consume bread and butter while taking the cure.

The elder

SACRED to the Druids and often found in votive pits – those deep holes which fulfilled a similar function to the votive bogs of the Norse gods.

Christian tradition holds that the elder is the ultimate in evil, asserting that it furnished the timber for the cross on which Jesus Christ was martyred and insisting that his betrayer hanged himself on one. The rubbery poisonous fungus frequently found growing on the elder is commonly called Judas's Ear.

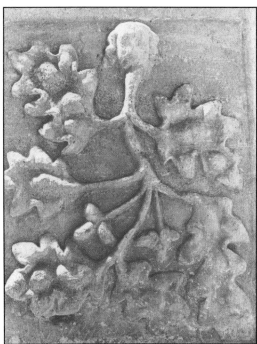

The Green Men on the font in the Church of the Assumption at Leckhampstead, Bucks, appear dwarfed by luxuriant vegetation.

The Old Religion returned philosophical fire, claiming that the elder was beneficent, that to mock it was to court misfortune.

The Church fearlessly countered that it was the tree of witches and to fall asleep in its shade invited recruitment; that the elder was a dormant witch as had been proved by wounds seen on witches when one was felled; and if one were cut on Midsummer's Eve it shed blood. To approach an elder after nightfall was unlucky.

It seems a drawn match. The belief survives that burning elder brings misfortune; others will not have it in the place at any price except in the form of elderberry wine which is popular with Christian and Druid alike.

The elm

A TREE notorious in tradition and folklore as the mortal enemy of man. Not only were coffins made of elm but it is noted for promoting business for itself by suddenly shedding a bough.

Wych elm did not derive from old hags on broom-sticks but from an old Saxon word which meant that it was pliable. This did not prevent 'picket-ty witch' entering the language as the name for a broom-aviator whereas it means 'three cornered field where the pliable elm stands.'

Walk nine times clockwise around an elm, place an ear to the bole and you will hear the Devil roaring. Some elms at St Austell, Cornwall, move about the field whenever the church clock strikes twelve. Twigs of wych elm will set butter on stormy days.

Hawthorn

FOR the Celts hawthorn was a powerful charm for good and had strong associations with May Day. Birch is considered a poor substitute for hawthorn as a maypole and if he knows what he is about Jack in the Green will arrive decked in its greenery. Hawthorn means spring is here and that summer is icumen in. It may not be brought indoors before May Day and some say not at all. A few sprigs hung outside protects against witches and lightning and a branch or so nailed to a byre door ensures a good milk yield. Under its other name of 'may' one is forbidden to cast clouts before it flowers on pain of a cold. It was once carried in wedding processions and branches were placed in coffins to ensure resurrection.

Miraculous hawthorn flourishes on Wearyall Hill at Glastonbury, said to have taken root from Joseph of Arimathea's staff thrust into the earth when he brought the Holy Grail from Jerusalem after the crucifixion of Jesus Christ. It flowers on the old New Year's Day and changes in the calender do not faze it.

Hazel
THAT a white serpent lives at the root of the hazel may be a confusion with the Norse tale of Yggdrasil, the Tree of Life. Hazel is sacred to the

Celts and frequently found in votive pits. Immensely useful for hurdles and water-divining although dowsers say that the power lies in the dowser not the bent twig. Of course, hazel keeps away witches and is often found growing near front doors.

Holly

HOLLY makes a good hedge and consequently good neighbours as they used to say in the country but misfortune will overtake those who trim it with the other species in the row.

An old tradition is that one cannot bring holly into a church before Christmas Eve nor should it be allowed to remain there after Twelfth Night. This stricture once applied to private dwellings. That witches hate it is a strong indication that it is a Druidical charm far older than its Christian association.

Rowan

SOME accounts – not all – say that rowan is one of the trinity of woods used by Druids to build sacred fires and it played an important role in their ceremonies but none of them mention exactly what that was.

That rowan is frequently found growing near standing stones is considered significant but that rowan gave protection against witchcraft might be a factor here. In northern England May Day bonfires were traditionally built of rowan branches.

Singing and dancing trees or standing stones

THOSE great monolithic icons of a dead religion should be inert but some swear they have life in them yet. They act differently for different people. They inspire a feeling of awe, they walk down to water to drink, or they dance and sing or make humming noises.

Venerable trees ape the stones. In the West Country, particularly pollarded oak and elm, with a board placed on top as a platform, were used for feasting and dancing and might be the root of this peculiar belief.

6

THE GREEN MAN IN LITERATURE

GREEN being the colour of most of nature it occurs so abundantly in literature that it is tempting to believe references to the colour are allusions or allegories concerning the Green Man and his obscure history. Often they are not. Some are are doubtful, others enigmatic and none more so than the mystical romance by a now forgotten author/knight who lived in the fourteenth century.

How green is his principle character? He could have equally been a brown or a red knight except that the narrative hints darkly at a far older time of spells and ritual, of an older religion, perhaps as incomprehensible to the unknown knight as it is to modern readers. The tragedy is that his source works are now lost.

Sir Gawain and the Green Knight is a tale told in the courtly style common to the Middle Ages with associations of chivalry, of damsels in distress and general derring-do but one senses undercurrents and the writer, not much more than a copyist, does not know what he is about. It is all rather like a man in full highland dress dancing the tango.

That the Green Knight gatecrashes King Arthur's court amid the joyful and carefree Christmas festivities to demand that someone hack off his head on condition that the swordsman submits himself to a similar fate in twelve months is rather pointless. The intruder confesses at a later stage that his mission was at the behest of Morgan the Fay, the magical half sister of the king himself and hints at sorcery but the reason is insubstantial. The subsequent bizarre adventures of Sir Gawain who witnessed his victim gather up his head and ride away after extracting the promise leaves the reader no wiser.

Understanding is not helped by the alliterative verse, not the modern

A knightly figure with sword and shield is on the spandrel of one of the four-teenth century choir stalls in Winchester Cathedral.

kind that gaily hurries a few words along but a stiff discipline of similar sounding syllables which hampers the flow of the story.

This antique style was open to Geoffrey Chaucer, a contemporary, but he wisely rejected it in favour of free prose with the result that the author of the *Canterbury Tales* is memorable while even the name of the writer of the Green Knight romance is unknown.

On his fatal final journey Sir Gawain meets and is given bed and board by his adversary (transformed for a while into a chivalric host) who strikes a nonsensical bargain with his lodger that whatever either receives becomes the property of the other.

Thus Gawain is the recipient of uneatable quantities of game from a compulsive hunter while he, formerly of flawless character, is tricked into breaking his pledge by concealing a jewelled girdle, a love token given him by his host's lusty and beautiful consort who three times attempts to seduce him. She extracts an oath that he will not betray her.

The venue of the fatal tryst, also the haunt of the Green Knight in his evil persona, is either a burial mound or passage grave near water which is cold but appears to boil. This magical spring was used in the Arthurian romances by Chretien de Troyes a century before. It is near a derelict chapel. He arrives to hear the daunting sound of a great axe being honed sharp on a grindstone.

After two false strokes of the axe, the third close enough to wound his neck and draw blood, Gawain lives on to the traditional happy ending and his joyous return to Camelot. The wounding was necessary, the Green Knight had explained, because of the broken pledge over the girdle, he being aware of the fleshy temptations offered by his wife from the first.

Only now, or so it seems, does it strike the narrator that he has written an account of a chivalric test for Sir Gawain but the almost palpable hesitation leaves one the sense that something remains hidden or unresolved and the weird and inexplicable symbolism (if it is such) poses questions without answers

The hue of the Green Knight, horse, armour, accoutrements, exceptionally a sprig of holly, that he normally inhabits a prehistoric grave near a church with a sacred well does suggest the Green Man dipped in Christian disinfectant but whether this is formal convention or deliberate association is open to conjecture until the unknown knight's unknown sources emerge.

Not so the legend of the Long Man of Wilmington, as old as England and there are no sources to be lost other than folk memory. Several independent authorities, one of them a modern and senior Druid, insist that the gigantic hillside figure was known throughout Sussex as the Green Man, not just because his chalk outline greened over naturally with lichen in sun and rain but the colour was intended by the ancient artist and never subjected to the annual, and ritual, scouring of other hill figures.

THE LONG MAN OF WILMINGTON
or a legendary tale retold

A WORKING windmill in a gale of wind is an awesome thing and not for timid folk. It has the power of a ship under sail but cannot make for harbour and must stand up to the tempest. The great sails beat like the wings of the Angel of Death, her timbers groan and her anguish enters the soul of all who hear her. Runner stone and bed stone roar and spark and her innards shrill and twitter like witches on Halloween. She tugs at her footings as if ready to fly up to the racing clouds and folk wonder why one never has.

A few still stand in quiet corners of the country and town folk come down at weekends and let the kids scream and holler at their feet, unaware of their terrible power. But most of them these days are skeletons, gutted, sweepless, flesh of rotted boards falling away into the nettles beneath. One or two are preserved and run long enough to grind little souvenir sacks of flour for the visitors to carry away with them. There is something different about this flour as if some magic has been implanted by the racing stones. Bread made from it tastes different, healthier, they say, not knowing that the real difference is the grit from the stones that will wear down molars as quick as chewing whetstones.

Even of a soft summer's day there is always wind where they stand, sometimes chill enough to send the old 'uns back to the car. This is not due to the ghost of some long dead miller although some might think so. Long deliberation, not chance, built the mill at that particular spot and the choosing was an ancient art and the possessor of the power was known as the Wind Smith.

Nature's steam to pant a windmill's engine is wind and wind is just like water. It will flow downhill and collect in pools and as a boulder changes the course and strength of a stream the broad green shoulders of the Downs are like rocks in the sough of wind. Wind holds close to frost like man to wife after Michaelmas but sun and furrow will shoot it skywards and so will the slopes of some hills and not others. Short turf pulls air down and sweeps it low into the Weald. There it bounces off stand of beech and oak, whistles about barn and rick, snakes along ancient hedgerows, dawdles in dell and hollow and chases like a hawk through coombe and valley.

All countrymen know about the queer ways of wind and some say the Wind Smith was no better than they, that his magic was no more than plain common sense plus knowing the lie of the land. But they said it quietly just in case he really was the Lord of the Winds and called down a tempest to lay their crops down.

Others believed he conjured up wind by sorcery, shaped it like a blacksmith does iron. Some believed he was was a priest of the Old Religion, even a god and they feared his wrath and power.

Even in the old days not many remembered the last Wind Smith for new mills were built where the old ones stood and these were sited when time was young. But it is said he always wore a wide-brimmed straw bonnet and a coarse woven smock that glowed white in soft sunlight. He had a garland of oak leaves about his thin neck and some were sure that his beard was of leaves too and so was his hair. Tall and thin like a thatching reed those that had dared to look into his face said it was wrinkled and of a high red colour with the noble dissipation of an old piper.

The eyes were green and watery like an old hen's and set deep under the leafy forehead and they had a distant look as if contemplating another age. He kept to himself, always alone stalking the high chalk, but sightings were rare. It was said that he survived on beech mast and took his drink from dew ponds. He spurned a roof but lived wild in the beech woods on the high slopes and sometimes sheltered in old shepherd's huts in harsh weather. He spoke to nobody, but he could be heard crying into the wind in a voice as shrill as a young crow's. He carried two long ash poles though some swore they were hazel just to know better. It was they who said his name was something like Dru. They also said that when casting a wind spell he clenched a leafy branch in his jaws.

When the monks built Wilmington Priory they needed a mill. The prior, an old man of much wisdom and holiness, thought it might be as well to invoke the offices of the Wind Smith. At this the sub-prior cried out in anger. He condemned the wanderer of the hills for not attending Mass, calling him blasphemer and the servant of the Devil himself. The old prior let him have his way..

The mill built, hoppers filled with grain, prayers said and hymns sung, the prior made the sign of the Holy Cross and with loud cheers from the villagers the miller-monk rammed in the striking rod. But the sweeps did not move which was uncanny for there was plenty of wind. The monks pushed and shoved and the wind blew harder but still the sails would not turn. The prior overruled his subordinate and despite loud lamentation sent a monk to find the Wind Smith who returned to say that he would come in a week to ten days which is an old English way of saying that he would come in his own good time. But, he had told the monk, there were to be no crucifixes or bells rung. ' They offend my eyes and ears,' he said..

' Proof that he is the Anti-Christ,' wailed the sub-prior.

' We must strive to live together in peace and harmony, brother,' said his old and gentle mentor.

Several breadless days passed before the Wind Smith strolled casually into the priory field. Without salutation or greeting he pushed a rod in here and sighted along it to the other there, stood on one leg, covered one eye and pointed his left arm and cackled a spell. He repeated the ritual many times throughout a long day and it was twilight before he pushed the last pole home, topping it off with the garland from about his neck.

'Here,' he croaked and strode off without another word. The sub-prior cried out that the new place was only a few paces from the old. But there was no help for it and the monks were put to rebuilding the mill.

There was great joy when the sweeps began to move and the sub-prior set up a clamour of bells that the earth shook. It was if a great hand had been laid on the sails for they beat slower and slower then stopped. Only when the peals died away would they turn again.

'We must ring the bells on the Lord's Day when the mill does not work,' counselled the old prior.

'The mill is evil,' cried his subordinate. ' Now we may only grind corn and ring our bells at the behest of the Devil.'

'May God bless us all,' said the old man, murmuring a paternoster.

Before that year ended the prior was called to his Maker and his junior appointed in his place. The Wind Smith's strange power over the mill still held sway and the new prior ground his teeth in fury. Then one day at prayer St Boniface came to him in a vision. Now this holy man was a wrathful and bitter opponent of the Old Religion, a destroyer of the sacred groves of the idolaters known as Druids in his native Devon. A monk was dispatched to entreat his intervention.

One morning at the Feast of Pentecost when the harvest had been gathered in there was the sound of singing like a visitation of angels. The prior looked out across the priory field to see a host in ecclesiastical vestments. At its head was a tall saintly figure in a mitre and he carried a golden crozier. From his vision he knew this was the great St Boniface.

'What's the problem?' asked the saint and the prior humbly explained his vexation. 'Have you a miracle about you?' he asked.

'It will require a very small one,' replied the saint loftily. ' We will begin with High Mass.'

And as the last voices died away Boniface ordered the bells to be pealed then he struck the sails three times with his crozier. There was a great rushing of wind and the whole windmill shook. Then slowly, very slowly at first, the sails began to beat the air.

'Hallelujah,' cried the monks. Faster and faster turned the sails and the stones began to smoke as the last grain drained from the hoppers. The monks toiled up the the ladders to replenish them and up and down until there were no more sacks to be emptied. The miller-monk wrestled with the striking road but it refused to budge. The sails spun faster and faster and the tortured stones screamed out and began to shoot out showers of sparks so that the risk of fire was great,

'Stop in the name of God,' cried Boniface in terror, beating in vain at the sweeps with his crozier. It was then they saw the Wind Smith hastening across the fields towards them.

'It is Satan's representative,' cried the prior.

'Keep back, Hound of Hell,' shouted Boniface in a great voice.

'As you wish,' replied the Wind Smith, resting on his poles to regard the saint's predicament at leisure.

'What can we do?' cried Boniface, capitulating at last for the mill was burning.

'We, Boniface? I very much doubt if "we" can do anything,' replied the Wind Smith cooly. ' But perhaps, I might.'

'You have come to mock me,' cried the saint.

'I came to help,' replied the Wind Smith.

'But are you not the Devil's servant? And is this not by his hand?' shouted Boniface.

'I am no more the Devil's servant than you. And are you not the Great Destroyer? Recall how you desecrated our sacred groves. Why it is that when your God casts down it is holy and when my kind build it is called evil?' asked the Wind Smith.

'Did you not conjure up this terrible wind? Is that not Devil's work?' Boniface retorted.

'Why should it be? Wind blows good as well as evil. And does not your God create all things?' observed the Wind Smith tartly.

'Your master's or mine, it makes no difference. Please call it off,' pleaded Boniface.

'Just reflect, my dear saint. If I do you will call it Devil's work. My kind will be always remembered for evil and yours for good,' said the Wind Smith.

'Stop the wind and I promise I will tell how you worked for the good of mankind,' cried the saint.

'Even saints make promises that are worthless when the danger is past,' persisted the Wind Smith.

'I swear by all that is holy that I know a way so that you will be remembered when I am dust and forgotten. Trust me, please trust me,' pleaded the saint.

'Hmm,' pondered the Wind Smith. Then at last he nodded and lay down down his poles. He gathered up his smock and began to run backwards. Three times he circled the blazing mill, running at a great speed, almost a blur to the watching monks. The wind calmed quickly, the sweeps ceased their wild rotation. The last zephyrs snuffed out the flames.

The Wind Smith wiped the sweat from his brow and picked up his poles. 'So be it,' he said. 'My day in done. The people are yours. Keep you promise and I will bother you no more.' He turned on his heel and walked away.

Nobody ever saw the Wind Smith again. And the saint was as good as his word. That day he set the monks to pull at the turf on the down above the priory to reveal the underlying chalk and the giant outline of the Wind Smith with his twin poles slowly took shape. He is there today and cannot be forgotten for he can be seen for miles across the Sussex Weald. He is called the Long Man of Wilmington which is a time-corrupted version of Windmill-tun or Windmill Hill. He, indeed, is remembered while the name of St Boniface, like he, is dust.

Reprobate Green Men struggling to escape from the Hell to which sin has brought them are on chancel arches in All Saints' church, Weston Longeville.

All too often missed by searchers in St Peter's church, Claypoole, are these early thirteenth century Green Men in stone capital friezes.

Mid fourteenth century roof boss in St Mary Redcliffe church, Bristol.

7

GREEN MAN GAZETTEER

PARLIAMENTARY tinkering with county boundaries has resulted in chaos for historians and map-makers alike. At the time of going to press there is a possibility that the old names will be restored. For this reason, with apologies, it is wiser and safer to use the original county names.

Although comprehensive the gazetteer is by no means exhaustive and the author will be delighted to receive additions from readers which will be published with due acknowledgement in future editions. The author wishes to thank members of the Company of the Green Man (see page 87) and other kindly readers who have contributed their discoveries to this new edition.

ENGLAND AND WALES
NDA = No date available

BUCKINGHAMSHIRE
Leckhampstead. Church of the Assumption. Font panel. Fourteenth century. **See page 66.**
Langley Marish. Church of St Mary the Virgin. Corbels. Fifteenth century.
CAMBRIDGESHIRE
Ely Cathedral. Roof bosses in the Lady Chapel. Date 1335–53.
Great Shelford. St Mary. Porch boss. Fifteenth century.

One of the two Green Men on the sixteenth century monument to Richard Harford and his wife in Holy Trinity church, Bosbury.

CHESHIRE

Astbury. St Mary. Roof boss. Fifteenth century. **See page 32.**

Nantwich. St Mary. Stained glass, capital, roof boss. Fourteenth century.

Chester Cathedral. Misericord. Date 1390.

St Kyneburga, Castor. Green Men of the twelfth century as pillar capitals.

CORNWALL

Lanreath parish church. Three roof bosses above altar. NDA.

Lostwithiel. St Bartholomew. Font. Fourteenth/fifteenth century.

DEVON

Bovel Tracy. Parish church. Frieze, porch, interior. NDA.

Broadnymet. St Martin. Roof bosses. Fifteenth century.

Budleigh. All Saints. Bench end 'Red Indian'. NDA/pre-sixteenth century.

Exeter Cathedral. Seventeen in all, in various settings. Thirteenth/fourteenth century. See pages 43 and 51

George Nympton. St Martin. Roof bosses. Fifteenth century.

Hobleton. Parish church. Chancel screen. NDA.

Kings Nympton. St Martin. Roof bosses. Fifteenth century.

Nymet Tracy. St Martin. Roof bosses. Fifteenth century.

Nymet Rowland. St Martin. Roof bosses. Fifteenth century.

Ottery St Mary. St Mary. Corbel. Fourteenth century.

Sampford Courtenay. St Andrew. Fourteen/fifteenth century rood bosses. See pages 56 and 87.

South Tawton. Roof bosses. Fourteen/fifteenth century. See page 56.

Spreyton. St Michael. Roof bosses. Fourteen/fifteenth century.

EAST SUSSEX

Alfriston. Star Inn. Roof beams above main door. Fourteenth century.

Winchelsea. St Thomas. Above tombs, south side. Fourteenth century.

ESSEX

Doddington. All Saints. Font. Fourteenth century.

Great Canfield. Parish church. South porch. NDA.

Great Dunmow. Parish church. North wall. Possibly fourteenth century.

High Easter. St Mary. Above door. NDA.

Little Dunmow. Parish church. Interior (unconfirmed). NDA.

Margaretting. St Margaret. Corbel ends near tower. NDA.

Matching. St Mary the Virgin. South wall corbel end. NDA.

Mountessing. St Giles. Nave central pillar. NDA.

Romford. Parish church. Rear wall. NDA.

Shenfield. St Mary. Font. Thirteenth century.

South Ockendon. Parish church. Wall east, on north door. NDA.

Stock Harvard. All Saints. Tower bosses and above priest's door.

Thaxted. St John the Baptist. South porch, south wall exterior, north transept, south transept wooden panel. Fourteenth century.

White Roding. Parish church. Horned god corbel, south side and end of chancel arch.

GLOUCESTERSHIRE
Bristol Cathedral. Vault bosses in Elder Lady Chapel. *c*1337.
Bristol, College Green. St Mary. Exterior wall. NDA.
Elkstone. St John. Tympanum. Twelfth century.
Gloucester Cathedral. Roof bosses, north transept and elsewhere.
Thirteenth century and later
Tewkesbury Abbey. Roof bosses. Fourteenth century.
GWENT (MONMOUTHSHIRE).
Llangwm. St Jerome's church. Corbel. Fifteenth century. **See page 8.**
Llantilio Crossenney. St Teilo's church. Wall carving.Fourteenth/fifteenth
century. **See page 42.**
Newport Cathedral (St Woloos) Font, Victorian/thirteenth century mix.
HAMPSHIRE
Winchester Cathedral. Fourteenth century choir stall spandrels. **See page 70.**
HEREFORDSHIRE
Abbey Dore. Ambulatory, screen, wall pintings. Sixteenth century.
Bosbury. Holy Trinity church. Monument. Sixteenth century. **See page 80.**
Garway Common. Chancel arch pillar. Thirteenth/fourteenth century.
Hereford Cathedral. Lintel carving. Fifteenth century. **See page 63.** Also
ambulatory, screen and wall paintings. Sixteenth century and earlier.
Kilpeck. St Mary and St David. Doorway. Twelfth century. **See page 48**
Much Marcle. St Bartholomew. Capitals. Date 1230-40.
Rowlstone. South doorway of church. Fourteenth century.
HUNTINGDONSHIRE
Castor, nr Peterborough. St Kyneburga. Capitals. Twelfth century. **See page 80.**
Bury, nr Ramsey. Parish church. Lectern. Fourteenth century.
KENT
Barfriston, near Dover. The church is a Romanesque gem. Musicians,
muzzled dog (more like a cat) people, faces. No Green Men sighted but a
possibility.
Canterbury Cathedral. Crypt pier capitals (particularly No 3), cloister roof
bosses. Twelfth century and later.
Rochester Cathedral. Painted roof bosses.
Rochester. Bank buildings in High Street. Victorian.
Sandwich. St Clement. Tudor font, foliage, Green Cats on tower crossing.
NDA.
Wade (Thanet). St Nicholas. Capitals (similar to Canterbury). NDA.
Wingham St Mary. Choir misericords depicting women, plants and flowers.
Fifteenth century.

A Green Man flouts authority with his tongue out from a fifteenth century roof boss in Crowland Abbey, Lincolnshire.

LANCASHIRE
Cartmel Priory. Choir stalls misericord. Fifteenth century. See page 33.
Whalley. St Mary and All Saints. Misericord. Fifteenth century.
LEICESTERSHIRE
Buckminster. Parish church. Porch and porch guttering. NDA.
Church Langton. St Peter. NDA.
Eastwell. St Michael. Porch corbel. Late thirteenth century.
Gadesby. St Luke. No information available.
LINCOLNSHIRE
Crowland Abbey. Roof boss. Fifteenth century. See above.
Harpswell. St Chad. Memorial dated 1350. See below.

The effigy of William Harrington, a former rector of St Chad's church, Harpswell, has a Green Man at its foot.

LINCOLN (Continued)

Lincoln Cathedral. Misericord on the choir stalls. Fourteenth century.

Cadney. All Saints. Corbels. Thirteenth century.

Claypole. St Peter. Capital. Thirteenth century. **See page 78.**

Grantham. St Wulfram. Corbel. Thirteenth century. **See page 18.**

NORFOLK

Kings Lynn. St Margaret. Misericord. Fifteenth century

Norwich Cathedral. Cloister roof bosses, misericord. Fourteenth/fifteenth century.

Weston Longville. All Saints. Sedilia arches. Fourteenth century. **See page 78.**

NORTHAMPTONSHIRE

Crick. Parish church. Five exterior carvings. NDA.

Wadenhoe. St Mary. Corbel. Thirteenth century. **See page 18.**

NOTTINGHAMSHIRE

Southwell Minster. Misericord, tympanum. Thirteenth/fourteenth century. **See page 29.**

OXFORDSHIRE

Dorchester Abbey, Corbel. Thirteenth century. **See page 19.**

Dorchester. Crown House (former inn) High Street. Door case.

Iffley. St Mary the Virgin. South door. NDA.

Oxford. Christ Church Cathedral. Latin chapel choir stalls. Fourteenth century.

SHROPSHIRE

Linley. St Leonard. Tympanum. Twelfth century.

Ludlow. St Laurence. Misericord. Sixteenth century.

Ludlow Castle. On wall north west of chapel. Possibly remains of upper room fireplace. NDA but probably medieval.

SOMERSET

Bath Abbey. Pew ends, chancel roof bosses. NDA.

Bishops Lydeard. St Mary. Bench ends. Fifteenth century. **See page 87.**

Bridgewater. St Mary. Main door, roof bosses. Thirteenth century (?)

Bristol. St Mary Redcliffe. Roof boss, stained glass, corbel. Fourteenth century. **See pages 13, 36, 59 and 79**

Crowcombe. Church of the Holy Ghost. Bench ends. Sixteenth century. **See page 26.**

Dunster. Parish church. Bench ends. NDA.

Glastonbury. St John the Baptist. Benches, north transept roof bosses. Date unknown.

Halse. St James. Roundel. Thirteenth century.

Kilton. Parish church. Capitals. NDA.

SOMERSET (CONTINUED)
Queen Camel. St Barnabus. Roof boss. Fourteenth century.
Wells Cathedral. Roof bosses. Fourteenth century. **See page 88.**
Wells. St Cuthbert. Porch and pulpit.
STAFFORDSHIRE
Burton-on-Trent. Town Hall. Victorian reproduction of older work.
Lichfield Cathedral. Capital. Date 1340. **See page 46.** Also choir and else-where. Fourteenth century.
Longdon. St James. Capital, doorway. NDA
Stafford. St Chad. Chancel, choir stalls. NDA
Enville. St Mary. Tomb.NDA
Gnosall. St Lawrence. Roof bosses, capitals. Date required.
Trysull. All Saints. (Reported but as yet not found).
SUFFOLK
Mildenhall. St Mary. Porch boss. Fifteenth century.
SURREY
Royal Surrey County Hospital. Chapel. Modern tapestries.
WARWICKSHIRE
Coventry. Holy Trinity. Misericord. Fourteenth/fifteenth century. **See page 40.**
WEST SUSSEX
Arundel Castle. Green Men carved on a Burgundian chest in baronial quarters. Bought in 1890 by the 15th Duke of Norfolk.
Boxgrove Priory, nr Chichester. Eight-faced roof boss. Fourteenth century.
Steyning. Post Office. Roof beam of Old Swann Inn. Seventeenth century. **See page 10.**
Chichester Cathedral. Modern altar painting and boss, third bay, south choir stall. Fourteenth century.
Jolesfield, nr Partridge Green. Modern *tete de fuille* pub sign. A recent replacement of the sign shown on the back cover.
WILTSHIRE
Bowerchalk. Holy Trinity. Chance roof bosses. Thirteenth century. And Victorian carvings (1865/66)
Devizes. St John. Capital near chancel. Fourteenth century.
Laycock Abbey. Cloister roof bosses. Tomb of Sir Walter Sherrington (1533).
Laycock. St Cypria. Lady Chapel arch.
Salisbury Cathedral. Misericord, roof bosses. NDA.
Salisbury. St Thomas. Capital near altar. NDA.
Sutton Benger. All Saints. Roof boss. Fourteenth century. **See page 22**

YORKSHIRE
Loversall. St Katherine Misericord. Fourteenth/fifteenth century. **See page 40.**
Ripon Cathedral. Corbel. Thirteenth century. **See page 19.**
Beverley Minster. Capital. Fourteenth century. **See page 46.**
Silkstone. All Saints. Roof boss. Fifteenth century.
Fountains Abbey. Window carving. Fifteenth century.

SCOTLAND

ROXBOROUGH Melrose. Abbey museum. Rood screen boss. Fifteenth century.

The spidery Green Man on a bench end at Bishops Lydeard which so resembles the one on a beam in the Post Office at Steyning, West Sussex.

SELECT BIBLIOGRAPHY

Anderson, W. *The Green Man*, Harper/Collins 1990

Basford, K. *The Green Man*, Brewer 1978

Blindheim, M. *Norwegian Romanesque Sculpture 1090-1210*. Taranti 1938

Caesar, Julius. *Gallic Wars*, various editions

Evans J. *A Study of Ornament in Western Europe 1180-1900*, Oxford, Clarendon 1931

Fraser, J. *The Golden Bough*, various editions

Fulconelli, A. *Master Alchemist: Le Mystere des Cathedrals*, Spearman 1971

Kidson, P. *Sculpture at Chartres*. Taranti 1958

Millar, R. *Will the Real King Arthur Please Stand Up?* Cassell 1978

Tacitus *Vita Agricola*, various editions

Sheridan, R. *Grotesques and Gargoyles; Paganism in the Medieval Church*, David and Charles 1975

Weir, A. *Images of Lust; Sexual Carvings on Medieval Churches*, Basford 1986

Young, B. *Villein's Bible; Stories in Romanesque Carving*, Bar

---

THE COMPANY OF THE GREEN MAN

If you have enjoyed this book you may like to join:

THE COMPANY OF THE GREEN MAN

Our newsletter welcomes your contributions. For
details please send stamped addressed envelope to:
Ronald Millar
The Tower, Wappingthorne Farm,
Horsham Road, Steyning,West Sussex BN44 3AA.
